Going Global

Roger Cartwright

T0341416

■ Fast track route to mastering globalization and successfully managing global expansion

■ Covers the key areas of global operations and globalization, from understanding cultural differences and global consumers to being global but acting local and understanding the social implications of globalization

■ Examples and lessons from some of the world's most successful global businesses, including Boeing, P&O and Sony, and ideas from the smartest thinkers, including Naomi Klein, David Korten, Richard Lewis, Michael Porter, Fons Trompenaars and George Yip

■ Includes a glossary of key concepts and a comprehensive resources guide

>>EXPRESS EXEC.COM<<
essential management thinking at your fingertips

Copyright © Capstone Publishing 2002

The right of Roger Cartwright to be identified as the author of this work has been asserted in accordance with the Copyright, Designs and Patents Act 1988

First published 2002 by
Capstone Publishing (A Wiley Company)
8 Newtec Place
Magdalen Road
Oxford OX4 1RE
United Kingdom
http://www.capstoneideas.com

All rights reserved. Except for the quotation of short passages for the purposes of criticism and review, no part of this publication may be reproduced, stored in a retrieval system, or transmitted, in any form or by any means, electronic, mechanical, photocopying, recording or otherwise, without the prior permission of the publisher.

CIP catalogue records for this book are available from the British Library and the US Library of Congress

ISBN 1-84112-316-1

Printed and bound in Great Britain by CPI Antony Rowe, Eastbourne

This book is printed on acid-free paper

Substantial discounts on bulk quantities of Capstone books are available to corporations, professional associations and other organizations. Please contact Capstone for more details on +44 (0)1865 798 623 or (fax) +44 (0)1865 240 941 or (e-mail) info@wiley-capstone.co.uk

Contents

Introduction to ExpressExec

ExpressExec is 3 million words of the latest management thinking compiled into 10 modules. Each module contains 10 individual titles forming a comprehensive resource of current business practice written by leading practitioners in their field. From brand management to balanced scorecard, ExpressExec enables you to grasp the key concepts behind each subject and implement the theory immediately. Each of the 100 titles is available in print and electronic formats.

Through the ExpressExec.com Website you will discover that you can access the complete resource in a number of ways:

» printed books or e-books;
» e-content – PDF or XML (for licensed syndication) adding value to an intranet or Internet site;
» a corporate e-learning/knowledge management solution providing a cost-effective platform for developing skills and sharing knowledge within an organization;
» bespoke delivery – tailored solutions to solve your need.

Why not visit www.expressexec.com and register for free key management briefings, a monthly newsletter and interactive skills checklists. Share your ideas about ExpressExec and your thoughts about business today.

Please contact elound@wiley-capstone.co.uk for more information.

Introduction to Going Global

» Many organizations are finding that global factors are impacting upon their operations.
» There are concerns by some that globalization by breaking down trade barriers and increasing the power of large companies may be detrimental to democracy.
» The sales of the largest multinational companies exceed the GDP of even quite well off countries.

In June of 2001 there were riots in the streets of Gothenburg, Sweden during a meting of the European Union (EU) held in the city. To compound the EU's embarrassment the meeting was also being addressed by the newly inaugurated US president, George W. Bush, who was making his first official visit to Europe. These riots followed disturbances in previous years at meetings of the World Trade Organization and other such bodies. The protests, which occurred in London, Prague and Seattle, were stated to be about the dangers of globalization.

Globalization is defined by Ellwood (2001) as "a new word that describes an old process: the integration of the global economy that began in earnest with the launch of the European colonial era five centuries ago. But (*sic*) the process has accelerated over the past quarter century with the explosion of computer technology, the dismantling of trade barriers and the expanding political and economic power of multinational corporation."

THE RELEVANCE TO INDIVIDUALS AND ORGANIZATIONS

The above might sound like a subject for economists, politicians and social scientists but of what relevance is it in a series such as *ExpressExec*?

More and more organizations, for reasons that will explored in this material, are reaching out to a wider, more global, marketplace. As this process increases in pace then an understanding of how globalization may affect business and the requirements of senior management to become global rather than local leaders is becoming a prerequisite as part of the strategy for an increasing number of organizations.

The riots and disturbances noted earlier had their roots in a belief that globalization was somehow replacing democracy with government by commercial organization or pan-regional governments. This belief is not confined to one end of the political spectrum. While some of the rioters were from the extreme left as are many of the academic critics of globalization, the militias in the US who appear to believe that the United Nations (UN) wishes to take over first the US and then the world are from the extreme right wing of politics. In the UK it appears that a majority of the right of center Conservative Party opposes a common European currency and the further political, social and economic integration that such adoption of the currency union would produce throughout the EU.

In other books in the *ExpressExec* series, Chapter 5 is concerned with the global implications of the subject. It is clearly difficult to have a chapter in this book concerned with the global implications of globalization for obvious reasons. In this book, therefore, Chapter 5 will examine the concerns of the critics of globalization, in particular the political and social implications. The chapter will attempt to explain why globalization appears to be such a danger to some sections of society as to bring people out onto the streets in violent protest.

The other chapters of the book will concentrate on how business organizations can expand into the global marketplace and how global factors are now impacting on even the most locally based enterprise.

GOING GLOBAL

Going global, in terms of this book is the process whereby organizations offer their products and services on a global rather than a local basis. The opportunities, threats and problems that this can present form the basis of Chapters 3 (concerned with the evolution of the process), 4, and 6 with Chapter 7 using case histories to bring out key insights.

While Ellwood (quoted earlier) states that it was Europeans who began the globalization process, in today's world they have been joined by organizations from other parts of the world. US organizations Ford, General Motors, Coca-Cola, IBM and Microsoft are just four of the large players, and from the Far East Sony, Hyundai, Mitsubishi, etc. have joined ICI (Imperial Chemical Industries) and P&O from the UK, Royal Dutch Shell from the Netherlands and Airbus Industrie, the pan-European commercial aircraft manufacturer.

It is salutary to note that according to the 1999 UN Human Development Program, the total sales in 1997 of General Motors, Ford and Mitsui were each greater than the Gross Domestic Product (GDP) of Saudi Arabia – an oil rich country (sales in US$: General Motors – $163bn, Ford – $147bn, Matsui – $145bn. GDP of Saudi Arabia – $140bn). Many multinational companies are now richer than whole countries.

What is Going Global?

» Going global is the process whereby organizations are able to offer their products and services across an increasingly wide geographic range.
» Globalization is the integration of the global economy by the dismantling of trade and political barriers and the increasing political and economic power of multinational corporations.
» Organizations tend to start local with growth moving along a regional–national–pan-national–international–global continuum.
» Organizations also tend to form alliances and partnerships abroad before moving into full international operations.
» Globalization is considered by some to present a serious threat and these concerns have been translated into violent protest.

Following on from the definition in the last chapter, going global has two dimensions. The first is the purely business one of expanding to serve a global customer base while the second is the effect of globalization in socio/economic/political terms to be explored in Chapter 5.

THE GLOBAL CONTINUUM

Consider a family-owned diner on Lexington Avenue in New York and a Macdonald's Restaurant in London. One is clearly local, the diner, and Macdonald's is a global operation. The difference is fairly easy to see. However, both may well be affected by the same global influences – the price of oil, rates of exchange. Both probably have local markets that they serve but both are in cities that cater for large numbers of tourists. Between them, along a continuum can be placed every business in the world. Some are purely local and some are clearly global. They can be classified as follows:

» Local
» Regional
» National
» Pan-national/bipolar
» International
» Global.

Local

Local businesses are just that. They operate in a very restricted area perhaps as small as a village. Many small enterprises begin as purely local operations. They often have a very loyal customer base and operate primarily in the domestic retail and service sectors providing local food outlets, household items and services such as plumbing. The trend has been for them to become squeezed by regional and national operations that can achieve economies of scale and thus charge less. Local operations can fight back by forming a consortium, e.g. the SPAR consortium of independent food outlets in the UK or by offering a more personalized service. Tied as they are to a restricted locality they are very vulnerable to fluctuations in the local economy. Through the use of the Internet (see Chapter 4) even the most local operation can now reach a much wider customer base.

Regional

Regional operations service a larger catchment area from a central location or have a chain of outlets etc. around the region. Regional organizations were very common at the time that transport systems, such as railways, were developing, but now can find it difficult to compete with larger competitors. Falling as they do between the ability of the local operator to offer a highly personalized service and the economies of scale that national and larger organizations can provide they can often be squeezed either out of existence or into mergers and takeovers in an attempt to build a suitable critical mass, i.e. a size that can compete.

National

An organization that has confined its main operation to a single country can be described as a national organization. Every country has them but care needs to be taken to ensure that the organization in question is truly national and not part of a larger global operation. For example, Ford have operations in the UK, Germany, and the US, but while they may be considered national by customers, those operations are part of a much larger global one.

National operations may have an international aspect in that they supply products abroad or purchase supplies from outside their boundaries. They may even have agencies abroad but if their core operation and staff are within one country they are national.

Pan-national

Increasingly national organizations are growing by becoming pan-national and setting up satellite operations abroad or securing strategic alliances with similar countries in other national areas. As Lorange and Roos (1992) have shown, these alliances often follow a particular life cycle of: ad hoc arrangements–joint project–consortium–full-blown joint venture. The end result can even be a merger.

In 1976, Eddy, Potter, and Page, writing about the airframe manufacturing market, commented that as far as the western world was concerned US hegemony in the market was inevitable. They pointed to the failure, as they saw it, of the relatively new Airbus Industrie to penetrate the market. A great deal changed in the quarter century since 1976.

Not only did the cold war end but Airbus were competing directly with Boeing (the market leader for much of the 1970s and 80s) on Boeing's home territory, the US, Boeing having by then absorbed McDonnell Douglas, its main US competitor. Airbus, as described by Matthew Lynn in *Birds of Prey – Airbus v Boeing* (1995), is a consortium of French, UK, German, Dutch, Belgium and Spanish manufacturers with its final assembly plant and headquarters at Toulouse in France.

In the automobile manufacturing industry such alliances have been quite frequent, often between a US and Japanese or European and Japanese manufacturer, or by an established manufacturer selling a complete obsolete production line to a partner, as Fiat of Italy did to Lada in the USSR.

International

The international organization is well on the way to becoming global. Such an organization is likely to have subsidiaries throughout the world.

At this stage the organization is still recognized as belonging to its country of origin and its satellite operations are likely to have much of the home base culture about them. Many airlines fall into this category. With deregulation of air travel, carriers are no longer restricted to picking up and landing passengers in their own countries. In the late 1990s British Airways (BA) took the decision to revise their livery so that the tailfins of their aircraft no longer reflected their UK origins but promoted a global impression. There was actually considerable customer resistance to this move not least in the UK and it has since been reversed but the idea was sound enough. BA wanted to be regarded as a global operation. This is difficult, however, if the name of the organization has the country of origin in the title. TWA (Trans World Airlines) perhaps had the right idea when they changed from Transcontinental and Western – the latter is regional/national, the former global.

Global

The global organization is one that, despite its country of origin being known, has developed the image of being from wherever it is operating. Coca-Cola is clearly a US product but consumers do not seem to consciously comprehend that. To many it is a local product because it is made and bottled locally and it is a global product because it is bought and consumed all over the world. Coca-Cola and its rival Pepsi Cola (Coca-Cola could have bought Pepsi in 1922 and decided not to) have the world market almost to themselves. The UK entrepreneur Sir Richard Branson launched his own product, Virgin Cola, in 1994 but it has not really impacted on the global Coke and Pepsi market share, a failure detailed by Tom Bower (2000). The story of Coca-Cola can be found in *For God, Country and Coca-Cola* by Mark Pendergrast (details in Chapter 9).

THE GLOBAL CONSUMER

There used to be a time, as recently as the 1960s and 70s, that a vacation abroad meant the opportunity to not only see new sights and experience different cultures but also to purchase products that one could not find at home. The same products (sometimes with a slightly different brand name, but the trend is to use common brand names if possible – it costs less) appear in stores from Sydney to Sunderland and from Tokyo to Turkey. The same music fills the air and the same fashions adorn the bodies. As will be shown in Chapter 4, the same software applications are carried on PCs that are clones of the IBM product. It is this commonality throughout the world that so worries the opponents of globalization who claim that traditions and heritage are being lost as everybody adopts a seemingly western lifestyle fueled by western advertising.

In fact they should be less worried than they appear because it is only in commerce that true commonality appear to have a basis. In other aspects of life, humans appear to be as divided as ever.

Mark Nicholson from the London Business School believes that although humans have evolved technologically, psychologically the species has not progressed very far from the tribalism of the Stone Age. In his *Managing the Human Animal* (2000), he makes a powerful case for this tension between what is technologically possible and the limitations of human psychological evolution. Lest anybody think that humans have advanced at the same rate psychologically as technologi- cally it is worth remembering events in Rwanda, Kosova and Bosnia Herzegovina at the end of the twentieth century and the appalling horror of the Nazi holocaust during World War II. Those events can only be understood from a tribal, group behavior viewpoint, as they do not fit into a global, homogenous world perspective.

The fact that they both wear Nike sneakers (trainers), Adidas tops and New York Yankees baseball hats will not stop two young men from across a sectarian divide hurling stones, petrol bombs and even bullets at each other. It may be a global world for products but it is still a divided one ideologically.

COMMONALITY AND DIVERSITY

In a world where the smallest retailer or manufacturer with a modem can reach across the globe, access to particular products and services is less restricted by barriers of distance or geography and only by the access customers have to the Internet, access that is growing daily. Software, music products and even the *ExpressExec* series can be delivered electronically (with safeguards to protect copyright and intellectual property). As will be shown in Chapter 6 however, consumers still consider a degree of diversity attractive and often require local adaptations to global products. Indeed achieving the required local diversity at a low cost may be the key to success for many organizations as they can then offer what the world wants with the diversity that the local requires.

The whole issue is complex. The following true anecdote illustrates this:

The author bought a new automobile. It was a Japanese brand but built in the northeast of England at one of the plants established by Japanese manufacturers to overcome the EU quota restrictions on Japanese automobile imports then in place. The author was berated by his neighbor, who had also recently purchased a new automobile, for buying Japanese and not British.

The neighbor had bought a Vauxhall Nova. For those not in the UK, Vauxhall is an old name in UK automobile manufacturing but has long been part of the General Motors (GM) conglomerate. Similar vehicles were sold in Germany under the Opel brand – another GM acquisition.

On the inside of the windshield of the neighbor's vehicle was a small sticker stating "Made in Spain." GM had relocated the Nova plant to Spain for economic reasons.

Who was the patriot? Was it the writer with a Japanese brand but built in the UK or the neighbor with a seemingly British car that was built in Spain for a US company?

KEY LEARNING POINTS

» Going global is a movement along a continuum from local to global via regional, national, pan-national and global.
» Strategic alliances and joint projects/ventures are part of the evolutionary process of going global.
» Globalization is a process that has political and sociological consequences as well as economic and commercial ones.
» Globalization is opposed by many who see it as a threat to traditions, heritage and even democracy.

The Evolution of Going Global

» The development of global organizations is not a new phenomenon.
» The British in India, J P Morgan and the US oil companies were pursuing global strategies long before globalization became an issue.
» Countries can be very concerned when their strategic assets are threatened by foreign ownership.
» The easing of barriers to world trade has been a major goal since 1944.

Globalization and the process of going global as described in this material began with the so-called voyages of discovery emanating in Europe from the fifteenth century onwards. While some of the explorers may have been concerned purely with extending knowledge about the world (a world many believed was, as taught by the Church, both flat and at the center of the universe–heliocentricity, the idea that the earth revolved around the sun was a heresy for which death by burning could be ordered), most were concerned with commerce – they were seeking new markets for their products and new products to sell on their home market.

These voyages were also responsible for the development of modern financing. They were a partnership between the explorer and those who risked not their lives but their capital on a successful venture. While the original ventures tended to be single projects with cargo and ship being sold off upon return to harbor, soon organizations, as we know them today, began to develop – organizations that had an existence that lasted longer than a single venture.

Most businesses anywhere in the world at the time were local, as the logistics for overland travel were difficult. European explorers soon came to find that they were not unique in the way they organized their economies and society as they discovered thriving civilizations in China, India and South America. Initially only in the case of the latter did the Europeans, driven by thoughts of gold and conversion to Christianity, seek to overthrow the rulers and take over. In respect of China and India the Europeans were content to set up trading stations in the coastal areas.

As sea travel was the easiest means of moving goods it is paradoxical that ports such as Bristol in England and the Hanseatic ports on the Baltic were international before they were national. The only national organizations until well into the sixteenth/seventeenth centuries were the ruler and the Church – the logistic of setting up national commercial organizations either in terms of transport or financing did not exist.

There were a number of commercial enterprises formed in Western Europe during the seventeenth and eighteenth centuries to further trade with both India itself and the East Indies. The companies, which had varying degrees of governmental support, grew out of the associations of merchant adventurers who voyaged to the East Indies following the discovery in 1498 of the Cape of Good Hope route by the Portuguese navigator Vasco da Gama. The most important of the companies were given charters by their respective governments, authorizing them to acquire territory wherever they could and to exercise in the acquired territory various functions of government, including legislation, the issuing of currency, the negotiation of treaties, the administration of justice, and even the waging of war; interesting comparisons with the complaints of some about modern globalization and the decline of government. The facts are that at the time there was no means that a European government could make its will felt thousands of miles away without a large navy, an army that could function in the heat and humidity of the tropics, and a great deal of expense. If private individuals were prepared to set up trade in these areas and finance the infrastructure, however, all the government had to do was provide a governor, a small number of "official" troops and an occasional visit by a naval frigate. The Danes, the Dutch (who held the Cape of Good Hope in modern South Africa at the time, and extended their interests throughout present day Indonesia, being a major power and influence in the area until well after 1945), the Portuguese in Goa (until removed by India in 1961), and the French all set up East India Companies but the most important was the company that received its charter from Elizabeth 1 of England.

ENGLISH (LATER BRITISH) HONOURABLE EAST INDIA COMPANY

The most important of the various East India companies, this company was a major force in the history of India for more than 200 years. The original charter was granted by Queen Elizabeth I on December 31, 1600, under the title of "The Governor and Company of Merchants of London Trading into the East Indies." At this time England and Scotland were two separate countries only being joined by a joint monarch (James 1 of England and V1 of Scotland) after the death of Elizabeth. The company was initially granted a monopoly of trade in Asia, Africa, and America but in practice kept its activities confined to India and the East Indies.

The company was managed by a governor and 24 directors chosen from its stockholders. In early voyages it penetrated as far as Japan, and in 1610 and 1611 its first factories, or trading posts, were established in India in the provinces of Madras and Bombay. Under a perpetual charter granted in 1609 by King James I, the company began to compete with the Dutch trading monopoly in the Malay Archipelago, but after a military defeat conceded to the Dutch the area became known as the Netherlands East Indies. Its armed merchantmen, however, continued sea warfare with Dutch, French, and Portuguese competitors. In 1650 and 1655 the company absorbed rival companies that had been incorporated under the Commonwealth and Protectorate by Lord Protector Oliver Cromwell after the English Civil War. In 1657 Cromwell ordered it to be reorganized as the sole joint-stock company with rights to the Indian trade. During the reign of Charles II, the company acquired sovereign rights in addition to its trading privileges, in effect it became the representative of the British Crown in India. In 1689, with the establishment of administrative districts called presidencies in the Indian provinces of Bengal, Madras, and Bombay, the company began its long rule in India.

The victories of Robert Clive, a company official, over the French at Arcot in 1751 and at Plassey in 1757 made the company the dominant power in India. With the French defeat at Pondicherry in 1761, the British and the Company were effectively the rulers of all India although native princes were allowed to keep their courts and rule as long as they followed British policies. It is interesting to see how, just as in North America the rivalry between Britain and France was fought out in India – a long way away from the European battlefields. The East India Company was the first instance of a modern global organization and its taking over of French possessions in India was the first example of warfare on a global scale, as Royal Navy vessels also took part in actions in addition to the Company's ships.

In 1773 the British government established a governor-generalship in India, thereby greatly decreasing administrative control by the company; however, its governor of Bengal, Warren Hastings, became the first governor-general of India. In 1784 the India Act created a department of the British government to exercise political, military, and financial control over the Indian affairs of the company, and during the next half century British control was extended over most of the subcontinent. In 1813 the company's monopoly of the Indian trade was abolished, and in 1833 it lost its China trade monopoly. Its annual dividends of 10.5% were made a fixed charge on Indian revenues.

The Company continued its administrative functions until the Indian mutiny of 1857-58. The catalyst for the mutiny was a concern that animal fats had been used to grease rifle cartridges. The cartridges of the time had to be bitten off before loading and such fats were considered unclean for religious reasons by many of the sepoys, as the native soldiers were called. However, the real cause was bitterness about the Company's handling of taxation and justice. Much savagery occurred on both sides before the mutiny was put down and in an attempt to prevent a repetition of the mutiny (by the Act for the Better Government of India 1858, the British Crown assumed all governmental responsibilities held by the company, and its 24,000-man military force was incorporated into the British army). The Company was dissolved on January 1, 1874, when the East India Stock Dividend Redemption Act came into effect.

The East India Company (John's Company as it was nicknamed) was the first example of an organization that was moving towards the more modern definition of a global one. Despite being confined in its trading activities to India, its influence as a commercial player was felt much more widely, to the East where it purchased goods and along the sea route back to the UK where its ships had to provision etc. By its involvement in the political and social life of India and its domination of the economy it was much more than just a business. In the modern world a large commercial organization can also dominate an area by virtue of its buying power and as will be shown in Chapter 5 can influence political decisions by its decisions to stay or relocate as a result of taxation etc. The East India Company in its heyday controlled no less than 50% of world trade and 25% of the world's population. Further details can be found in the East India Company by Anthony Wild (details in Chapter 9).

THE INDUSTRIAL REVOLUTION

The industrial revolution that began in the UK at the beginning of the nineteenth century was a time when local organizations and companies had the opportunity to become national. The building of a rail network, first in the UK and the eastern seaboard of the US and then throughout

Europe, ensured that goods and people could be transported swiftly and safely in a fraction of the time previously possible. From a twenty-first-century viewpoint, with aircraft travelling at anything up to twice the speed of sound, it is perhaps difficult to comprehend the difference that rail travel brought, especially in Europe where distance between major population and manufacturing centers are less than in the US. By 1888 the average speed on the UK's Great Western Railway was 46mph with that company's loco, the City of Truro, registering the first recorded speed over 100mph in 1904. By 1890 the UK rail network was complete and there were few, if any, towns or even villages more than 5 miles from the nearest station except in more remote areas. In 1865 at the end of the Civil War there were 35,000 miles of track in use in the US, by 1888 this number had increased by a factor of over 4 to 156,000. The national expansion of large organizations was now possible. The railroads themselves, together with the shipping companies that were moving increasing numbers of emigrants across the Atlantic, were among the largest of these new industrial giants, as were the iron and steel works, mining, engineering, and chemical plants that were being developed at an increasing rate.

Originally national in nature, it was a long time before growth outside national boundaries was contemplated. Imperial powers of which the UK was by far the largest could expand into their colonies. The introduction of cotton weaving into India by UK entrepreneurs eventually led to the downfall of the home industries in the north of England after 1945 because they could no longer compete on price.

J P Morgan

The first of the twentieth-century global operations, however, was masterminded from the US by the financier J P Morgan using the financial power of the Morgan Guarantee Trust. A banker and venture capitalist, by 1900 Morgan controlled a number of the most important US railroads and was later to help form the mighty US Steel Corporation. A philanthropist and collector of important works of art, Morgan was also a ruthless businessman, a facet of his nature shown quite clearly in the operations of the IMM (International Mercantile Marine Company). Ostensibly IMM was a UK operation run by the chairman of the White Star Line, J. Bruce Ismay. In reality IMM was controlled and financed by Morgan from the US with the objective of gaining a monopoly of the lucrative transatlantic passenger traffic. That traffic included the transportation of emigrants from Europe to the US and the trade used the largest liners yet seen in the world. Morgan had attempted to acquire two German companies but had failed and he then turned his attentions to the UK giants of Cunard and White Star.

Shipping was the most important factor in world trade (in many ways it still is). France, and later the UK, had sponsored and supported the building of the Suez Canal in the latter years of the nineteenth century and the US considered the Panama Canal, opened in 1914, as part of its strategic interest, even to the extent of purchasing the Danish Virgin Islands in the Caribbean (St Thomas etc.) to guard its Atlantic end.

Morgan acquired interests in White Star and a number of other UK and European shipping lines and then tried to buy Cunard but was thwarted by the UK government. He was helped in his acquisition by the chairman of the Harland and Wolff shipbuilders in Belfast, William (later Lord) Pirrie. Harland and Wolff built all of White Star's ships and thus stood to gain by accessing Morgan's money for ships that they would then build on a building cost plus commission basis (Harland and Wolff could not lose on such an arrangement as their costs would always be met in full). Under Morgan's invisible control they built the *Titanic* and her two sisters – the *Olympic*, which had a long and successful career, and the *Britannic*, which sunk in World War I while serving as a hospital ship.

It is therefore a little known fact that the infamous *Titanic*, well known for sinking on her maiden voyage after colliding with an iceberg in April 1912 was actually ultimately owned by a US company. She might have flown the blue ensign (her captain was an officer in the Royal Naval Reserve and thus entitled to fly the blue and not the red ensign), be officered and crewed almost entirely with UK citizens, be registered in Liverpool and owned by the apparently British White Star Line but she was in fact the property of J P Morgan and the Morgan Guarantee Trust. Morgan was due to sail on her maiden voyage and cancelled at the very last minute – history might have been very different had he been on board. More care might have been taken and the ship would now be just a footnote in history books.

The loss of the *Titanic* and subsequent losses in World War I denied him his ambition on the global stage but it is interesting to note that few on either side of the Atlantic were aware that a US financier had acquired no fewer than five UK and one Belgian shipping companies including White Star and its large fleet of passenger liners. When the UK government realized that as a maritime nation part of its strategic reserve was under the control of a foreigner, it acted immediately to subsidize Cunard to build the record breaking *Mauretania* and her ill-fated sister the *Lusitania*, torpedoed and sunk in World War I with a terrible loss of life. Part of the subsidy was a requirement that Cunard must remain British, a condition not changed until Carnival (started by the US entrepreneur Ted Arison in 1972 with one ship and now the largest cruise company in the world) acquired the Cunard brand and its ships in 1998.

Had World War I not broken out there is a considerable likelihood that Morgan's global ambitions would have increased and that might well have started the process of globalization as it is known today decades earlier that it actually began.

Between the wars

World War I put the expansion plans of many companies on hold, those of companies located in the Triple Alliance (Germany, Austro-Hungary, and Turkey) Krupp, I.C. Farben, Skoda etc. to be shelved for decades. The war had a dramatic effect, however, in shifting the nature of the basic world economy. Prior to 1918 the world was a coal-based economy, thereafter and through to the present day it has been oil-based. The launch of the battleship *HMS Queen Elizabeth* in October 1913 was the commencement of a new era. Prior to this all of the Royal Navy's (and the rest of the world's) warships and all merchant ships had been coal fired. This meant that huge quantities of coal had to be carried and the dirty and backbreaking task of coaling ship – mainly by hand, as the coal was poured down narrow shoots into the bunkers – had to be carried out every few days. In World War I the British Grand Fleet (just part of the Royal Navy) used 100,000 tons of coal per week. The Grand Fleet was stationed in Scapa Flow in the Orkney Islands off the North of Scotland and the movement of so much coal to such a remote spot put a huge strain on the UK's railways and the single line that led up to that part of Scotland. The UK had massive supplies of good steam coal, however, and was thus self-sufficient. As the major maritime nation in the world at the time, much of the UK's colonial expansion post 1850 had been in the setting up of coaling stations along her sea routes.

HMS Queen Elizabeth and her four sisters were not only the Royal Navy's largest and fastest battleships, they were also oil-fired. The *Queen Elizabeth* had a silver shovel mounted on her superstructure to remind the crew of what they were being spared. Oil is not as heavy as coal and thus the weight saved can be put to good use as armor, and it is paradoxically less explosive. Empty coal bunkers contain fine particles of residue that are easily ignited. It was once thought that the *Lusitania* (see earlier) was carrying clandestine explosives that were set off by the torpedo that hit her. It is now believed that there was a sympathetic explosion of coal dust residue in an empty bunker and that this is what caused the tragedy.

Moving to oil fuel for the Royal Navy was a tremendous risk as at the time the UK had no oil supplies of its own (it is now the largest producer of oil in the EU as oil has been discovered all around the coast especially in the North Sea). However the experiment was a success and all future warships and merchant ships were oil fired or even diesel powered thus dispensing with steam altogether. Older tonnage was converted and only the railways and power stations remained dependent on coal. The leaders in the new global economy would depend on securing sources of oil of which the US and the then neglected Middle East had an abundance.

The US government that had been so suspicious of trusts and cartels before the war now began to secure the nation's supplies by encouraging such syndicates of oil companies. Collier and Horowitz (1976) have commented that the US government was actually orchestrating the formation of a powerful syndicate of US oil companies abroad. Whereas in the past such syndicates would have been illegal, the government refused to assist Standard Oil in expanding into Mesopotamia on its own.

The UK was also encouraging its oil companies to explore foreign fields and ensure that they controlled not only the oil but also the policies of the governments beneath whose land it lay. Many of the German, Italian and Japanese strategic problems in World War II lay in their lack of a friendly supply of oil and their need to try to take oil by force, thus removing military forces from other objectives. Germany's only friendly source of oil was in Romania and those were not large reserves and were vulnerable to air attack.

The world was hit by the great depression between the wars and many smaller companies were taken over, the foundations for the future giant multi-nations were being laid.

Post 1945

The US emerged out of World War II as the major economic force in the world. Europe and Japan had been devastated by bombing with many vital industries destroyed. The UK had escaped invasion but had been heavily bombed and was near to bankruptcy. The US had not been bombed and US industry had prospered. Only the US had the industrial capacity to provide the goods so vitally needed to rebuild the world. The excess capacity needed in wartime was tasked to the process of rebuilding through initiatives such as the Marshall Plan, and the Cold War meant that the military manufacturers did not have to completely scale down as had happened in 1918.

In 1944 the Bretton Woods conference in New England brought together 44 nations (associated with the Allies) to discuss the economic shape of the post-war world. The conference was centered on the concept of free movement of goods backed by the US dollar as an international currency. The results of Bretton Woods have been far reaching, leading to the setting up of the International Monetary Fund.

The International Monetary Fund (IMF)

Acting as a lender of last resort, the IMF, to which members contribute, will lend money to governments to assist them out of crisis. Very strict conditions, usually related to levels of public spending, are attached to the loans. Part of the IMF rationale is that if an economy collapses, this will have implications for all economies and must thus be prevented.

The World Bank (International Bank for Reconstruction and Development)

Working alongside the Marshall Plan of the US, the World Bank provided money to assist post-war reconstruction, and latterly has lent below market rates to assist the poorer governments to carry out major capital projects that will benefit their economies.

General Agreement of Tariffs and Trade (GATT)/World Trade Organization (WTO)

GATT was established to set up rules for the governance of world trade and to promote the free movement of goods and services without tariff barriers. In 1994 the WTO was established as an international organization to pursue the concept of free trade. It settles trade disputes that allow the aggrieved member to place restrictions on goods of an offender.

In 2000 the WTO ruled in favor of the US over preferential imports of bananas from ex-Caribbean colonies into the EU. The US then threatened to place tariffs on certain goods, e.g. Scottish cashmere imported from the EU into US. This would have devastated the economy of the Scottish borders region and manufacturers there rightly complained that their futures were being jeopardized over Caribbean bananas (see Ellwood, 2001). As in the majority of such cases, a compromise was agreed ending the "banana war" in June 2001. The EU argued that such restrictions deny sovereign governments the ability to take decisions based on national interest.

Of current concern is the WTO rules that try to force countries to take foodstuffs that they believe may be hazardous due to the addition of hormones or genetic modification. When the EU protested that hormone-fed beef was illegal in Europe, the US took the EU to the WTO and received a favorable ruling with the result that the US applied 100% tariffs to certain EU food products.

Fig. 3.1 provides a time line for the globalization process.

As will be shown in the remaining chapters of this material, the growth of global trade and organizations operating on a global basis has been massive since 1945. The same clothes, foodstuffs, soft drinks, alcoholic drinks, automobiles and aircraft are seen in every corner of the globe. News organizations, such as CNN, reach more and more homes and the Internet (see Chapter 4) makes a mockery of the barbed wire and watchtowers of some national borders.

Economic groupings, the European Union, and NAFTA (North American Free Trade Agreement) are breaking down previous political,

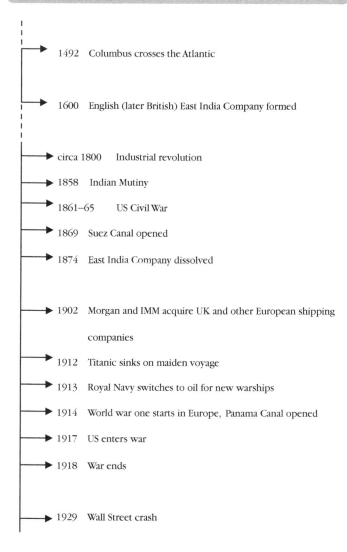

Fig. 3.1 Time line for the evolution of globalization.

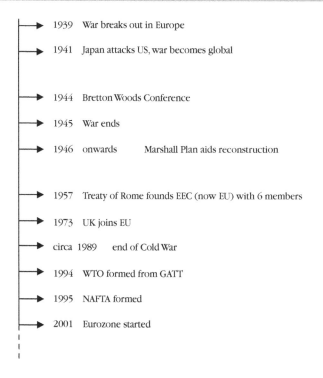

1939   War breaks out in Europe

1941   Japan attacks US, war becomes global

1944   Bretton Woods Conference

1945   War ends

1946   onwards   Marshall Plan aids reconstruction

1957   Treaty of Rome founds EEC (now EU) with 6 members

1973   UK joins EU

circa 1989   end of Cold War

1994   WTO formed from GATT

1995   NAFTA formed

2001   Eurozone started

Fig. 3.1 (*Continued*).

economic, and trade barriers. Despite this opening of the world to trade and global organizations, however, famine and war are still all too common in many areas. That is perhaps the next big challenge for globalization.

KEY LEARNING POINTS
» Governments will act so as to protect strategic assets from foreign ownership.

» Governments will assist companies is acquiring control of strategic resources such as oil.
» Once a company becomes involved in another country in a major role it also becomes involved in the politics etc. of that country.
» Since 1945 the move has been towards free trade and economic blocs such as the EU and NAFTA.

Implications of the Internet for Going Global: What Can the Internet Offer?

» The Internet and e-mail have revolutionized global communications.
» The Internet allows even the smallest organization to reach a global customer base.
» It is harder for governments to censor Internet material than any other form of news or communications.
» The ability of linked computers to aid design and manufacturing as shown in the case of the Boeing 777 has allowed new and more efficient forms of cross-border cooperation.
» Products for the Internet belong, in a way, to the whole world rather than to one country.

Basically the Internet is a network of linked computers that can be accessed from any remote site using another computer and a modem. All kinds of information can be placed on the computers of the network. These servers hold the information in the form of Web pages each with its URL (Uniform Resource Locator) that can be opened either by anybody or by specified people in possession of a password. Users of the Internet do not even have to know the URL as there are a number of search engines such as Lycos, Yahoo!, Excite etc. that will search the Internet for a user and find all the sites that match the keywords that they have been requested to find. The Internet is also a vehicle for electronic communication either by text e-mail or videoconferencing. There are thus a number of ways that the Internet can impact the process of organizations expanding globally.

Much of this chapter will be taken up with a case study that shows how the use of information and communication technology (ICT) has changed the way organizations can operate on a global arena. The case study relates to the planning, design and building of the Boeing 777 airliner. Boeing may be situated in Washington State but the designs and components came to final assembly from across the world. What made this of interest in this material is that much of the design work was undertaken using linked computers allowing what happened in Japan or the UK, or other parts of the US to be directly controlled from Seattle.

HOW THE INTERNET CAN AID ORGANIZATIONS OPERATING IN A GLOBAL ENVIRONMENT

The rapid growth in the Internet has brought about a situation where markets are no longer constrained by geography. As more and more organizations trade online and as customers become comfortable with browsing the Web for purchases and undertaking online financial transactions, the concept of a local supplier has been diminished.

Amazon.com (a case study subject in Chapter 7) has revolutionized book and music sales. Even on a national basis (Amazon has warehousing in countries other than the US to cater for local deliveries) they allow those in remote areas to purchase books from their computer at home with speedy delivery using the mail. Motorists in the UK can purchase vehicles from other EU countries (where they have tended to be cheaper) and even arrange delivery at a cost. What was started as mail order to satisfy settlers in the US during the settlement of the areas west of the Mississippi towards the end of the nineteenth century is now a hi-tech means of searching the world for goods.

Communications

Organizations operating on a global basis can use the Internet and e-mail to simplify the communication process. Where once it took days for a document to be taken from Europe to the US it can take a fraction of a second. Videoconferencing through systems such as Microsoft Windows® and the Internet can be undertaken from any location with a telephone connection. E-mail can be picked up from any location and there are cybercafés in most large population centers that allow visitors to access the Web and pick up their e-mail. All of this means that corporate control is much easier and that policies etc. can be speedily disseminated throughout an organization.

News is also easier to obtain and government censorship much harder. Totalitarian regimes may be able to control traditional media but the control of Internet news is much harder if not impossible. That some censorship is necessary to protect against pornography, for example, cannot be denied but it requires cooperation between Internet companies and governments and not unilateral action.

The communications available to the modern organization would have seemed like science fiction as late as the early 1980s. Almost any organization that wishes a global customer base can have one. If its products and services can actually be delivered over the Internet, for example text, music, financial services, entertainment bookings, software etc. (provided of course that there are no copyright infringements) then the virtual organization with savings in facilities costs is now no longer science fiction but science fact.

Microsoft, Lotus, Norton etc., Internet Service Providers (ISP) such as AOL (America On Line) and search engines – Lycos, Yahoo!, AltaVista, Excite etc. have global names almost overnight because of the global nature of their product. Their corporate headquarters may be in a particular country but in many ways they belong to the whole world.

Bill Gates of Microsoft may be the most powerful person on this planet as his products are among the most important tools used by business and governments. Whether one approves or disapproves, and the US government is certainly concerned about the monopoly power of Microsoft, we live in a Microsoft-dominated world with more people using Microsoft Windows® than perhaps any other consumer brand.

BEST PRACTICE

Boeing, the 777, DBTs (design build teams), CATIA (computer graphics-aided three-dimensional interactive application) and EPIC (electronic preassembly in the CATIA)

The world famous Boeing Aircraft Corporation has been headquartered around Seattle (WA) since its founding by Bill Boeing in 1917. Since then it has grown dramatically. By the 1930s it was a conglomerate that included not only Boeing Aircraft but also Boeing Air Transport, United Air Lines, Pratt and Whitney (still one of the major aero engine manufacturers) and Hamilton Standard Propellers.

Unfortunately the regime of F.D. Roosevelt's first term was very much anti-trust and against huge conglomerates so that Boeing was broken up into its constituent parts. Interestingly, Boeing, United Airlines and Pratt and Whitney were to come together again for the Boeing 777. Boeing made the plane, the engines for the prototype were two Pratt and Whitney 4080 powerplants (although General Electric and Rolls Royce engines are also available to meet customer requirements) and of the two launch customers for the aircraft one was the US carrier, United Airlines, and the other for British Airways.

By the time the 777 was under consideration in the early 1990s, Boeing had an excellent track record of producing jet transports. The Boeing 707, 727, 737, 747 (Jumbo), 757 and 767s were familiar sights on the runways of the world's airports. Their main US rivals, Lockheed and McDonnell Douglas were unable to compete with Boeing (McDonnell Douglas being acquired by Boeing in the

1990s) and only the European Airbus Industrie were selling an equivalent volume of airframes.

It was deemed that the airline world was ready for a large twin-engined airliner capable of performing on long-haul sectors. The use of two engines cuts the costs of both purchase and operation considerably but requires a high degree of reliability. The 777 was the first airliner to be built to gain ETOPS (extended twin-engine operations) by the Federal Aviation Administration (FAA) from its introduction. Previous twin-engined jets had always to fly within 60 minutes of a landing site for two to three years to assess the reliability of the engines before ETOPS was granted. This cut out many over-water routes.

A twin-engined airliner offering a range of 5,500–7,000 nautical miles and carrying 300–400 passengers was likely to be very attractive to the world's airlines especially as it was predicted to be very fuel efficient.

A modern airliner is a highly complex machine requiring a considerable number of carefully engineered components. Manufacturers such as Boeing now contract out a great deal of the component manufacturing. This has the advantage that the contractor has to bear the start up costs but the disadvantage that Boeing have to make their proprietary information available to an organization that may also be working with a competitor or may actually become a competitor in the future. Nevertheless, it has proved more effective for companies such as Boeing to work this way and involve others in the process.

For the 777 the manufacture of components was spread across the world as shown by the sample below:

» Outboard flaps: Italy
» Passenger doors: Japan
» In-spar ribs: Japan
» Elevators: Australia
» Rudder: Australia
» Many fuselage sections: Japan
» Spar assembly tool: Wisconsin (US)
» Prototype's engines: Connecticut (US)

» Nose: Kansas (US)
» Fuel gauges: UK
» Entertainment system: UK.

Eddy *et al.* (1976) report that when Lockheed and Rolls Royce were collaborating on the Tri-Star in the 1960s and 70s (an airline that used the Rolls Royce RB211 engine), Rolls Royce engineers were to be seen flying across the Atlantic to take metal ducting designed in Derby to Burbank to see how it fitted on the aircraft and how it would perform. This was both time consuming and expensive. Modern technology allowed Boeing to link their designers to the contractors and even to the actual machine tools.

One of the problems in designing something as complex as an airliner is that of interference – two components trying to occupy the same space. In the days of two-dimensional drawings this was an all too frequent occurrence. Computer-aided design (CAD) can produce drawings in three dimensions and thus show the relationship in space between components.

Boeing put together a massive amount of computer power in a system known as CATIA (computer graphics-aided three-dimensional interactive application) and EPIC (electronic pre-assembly in the CATIA). EPIC allowed a computer model of the finished aircraft – a virtual airliner – to be produced. CATIA was linked to component manufactures so that the specification of parts designed on the system were immediately available to them and could be fed, if necessary directly to the machine tools.

Aircraft design is a process rather than an event and there are often many design changes. Before systems such as CATIA, these might be posted, faxed or even hand delivered. With the system used by Boeing, everybody concerned with that component would know of changes as soon as the new design was on the system. The time savings were immense.

As EPIC could spot any interference, it meant that the finished product was much more likely to fit together properly than it did. The whole process was documented in an excellent book – *21st Century Jet* by Karl Sabbach – and also in a joint US/UK television series. Sabbach reports how the computer checked for interferences on the 20 components that make up one of the 777's wing flaps. It made 207,601 checks and found 251 cases of interference. These might not have been discovered under the old system until an attempt was made to install the flap on the prototype, any problem then forcing the designers back to their drawing boards.

Each component or major group of components was the responsibility of a DBT (design build team) that could include remote members as the Internet, and ICT made e-mail and videoconferencing an easy and useful tool.

No longer did designers have to take their drawings or models to a colleague on another floor or even another city or continent to see if it was OK. The whole process could now be carried out over a network of computers. While this has not been an application much quoted, it must be one of the most important and groundbreaking uses of networks in recent time, holding forth as it does the prospect of global cooperation on design and manufacturing without any of the problems of distance, geography, or time. No longer do designers have to waste precious hours on travelling.

The DBTs also formed a forum not only for discussion but ownership of a component. By using the technology to involve team members at remote locations, everybody was involved. This is an important motivational point often neglected when subcontracting. The further away the sub-contractor's staff are, the less likely they are to feel part of the team and thus to own the project. Ownership gives a huge boost to quality.

While Boeing set up a special bank of computers to handle the huge amounts of data, smaller projects can use these concepts with PCs etc.

By feeding information from CATIA into EPIC, it was possible to see exactly how the airline would appear and this also made the task of simulating its performance easier. In fact so good was the design that the 777 was even more fuel efficient than predicted and it did become the first airliner to achieve an ETOPS rating at its introduction.

A great deal of the initial success of the 777 must be put down to the use Boeing made of ICT and the way they used technology not only to overcome technical design and manufacturing issues but to involve what was a global operation in considerable detail.

Sabbach presents the story in a non-technical manner and is thus well worth consulting by those interested in how huge global projects such as the 777 are managed.

KEY LEARNING POINTS

» The whole means by which communications are handled has been revolutionized by the Internet.

» The linking of computers allows for new forms of cross-border projects and cooperation.

» The whole world can be your customer if your products and services are online.

» The virtual, Internet-based organization without any geographical or space constraints is a reality.

» The Internet makes censorship impractical without global consent.

The Issue of Globalization

» Globalization has opponents who are worried about its economic effects and the decline of democracy.
» Some organizations, termed "swallows" move from one low-cost economy to another, depriving areas of income and job security.
» Consumer resistance to child labor and exploitation is growing and has led to boycotts.
» Democracy can be threatened if the concerns of special interest groups are put above those of the general population.

To the man or woman in the street, the riots at recent meetings of world leaders in Prague, Seattle, and Gothenburg may seem inexplicable. To many in the developed world, globalization has brought immense benefits, not least in providing free access to a huge range of consumer products. At a time when ethnic divides seem as great as ever there is perhaps superficial comfort in the fact that we all seem to drink the same sodas, watch similar television programs on similar televisions, listen to similar music and eat foods far more exotic than those enjoyed by previous generations.

To the opponents of globalization, however, the issues are far deeper and center around the removal of fiscal and political independence from governments and the apparent transfer of power to the larger corporations in the world. To such opponents, globalization is more than just similar products being available on a global basis. To them it is actually the integration of the global economy by the dismantling of trade and political barriers and the increasing political and economic power of multinational corporations.

An increase in trade should benefit everybody. According to Ellwood (2001), world trade is increasing at around 6% per annum. As David Ransom (2001) writing in the same series points out, however, the increases are less beneficial unless the trade is actually fair, which he believes in the vast majority of cases it is not. If the result of an increase in trade is actually a decrease in living standards throughout a proportion of the world as a result of manufacturers cutting wage rates to gain orders, then the benefits of trade become lost to the very people who should gain – those producing the goods.

From the point of view of an individual citizen, government must seem huge and governments have been growing in size and activity throughout the past 200 years. Governments in 1800 were small in comparison with their modern successors, as of course were populations. Social policy and intervention were in their infancy and for many people the government hardly influenced their lives directly from birth to death – a majority did not even pay income taxes. A modern government, however, even in the most non-interventionist regime – the US – still has a large direct influence over daily life, not least through direct and indirect taxation and the administration of a welfare system.

However, not all governments and economies are as large as the US, the UK, Germany, France or Canada etc. Ellwood states that of the 100 largest economies of the world, multinational corporations account for 50%. In fact according to the United Nations Development Program report of 1999, the "Economy" of General Motors is larger than that of Norway, a European nation although not an EU member, and considerably larger than that of Greece, a country that is an EU member. It is somewhat staggering that not only General Motors but also Ford, Mitsui, Mitsubishi, Itichu, Shell, and Mauruberi *each* has sales revenues greater than the Gross Domestic Product (GDP) of Greece. Perhaps even more surprising is that the sales revenue of Wal Mart exceeded the GDP of Israel by about $10bn in 1997, a figure that has doubtless increased since Wal Mart acquired the UK supermarket giant Asda in 2000.

ATTRACTING COMPANIES

Just like individuals countries have to earn money before they can spend it, in order to acquire goods and services from outside their own borders it is necessary to earn foreign currency. The USA, UK, Germany etc. - i.e. the developed nations - are able to earn foreign currency using a mixture of exporting raw materials and manufactured goods and by providing services to other countries. Many developing countries are more dependent on raw materials and are particularly vulnerable to a fall in prices if they are dependent on a single resource or crop. Earning foreign currency by providing services requires the development of expertise which can take a great deal of time, and therefore the development of a manufacturing capability is seen as a useful addition to the economy as it lessens the dependence on a small number of raw materials or crops.

Governments welcome manufacturing companies because they not only provide goods for export in many instances but because they provide employment. No government can afford to ignore the social condition of its citizens for long - to do so is likely to lead to the fall of the government through elections in democratic regimes and revolution in totalitarian ones. A government must be seen to be assisting people with jobs especially if the economy is stagnant and there is high unemployment. High employment rates mean that the government has to do relatively little but once the unemployment rate begins to rise the population require action.

This is not a new concept. In the 1930s both Theodore Roosevelt in the US and Adolph Hitler in Nazi Germany began huge public works' programs to put people back to work in order to beat the effects of the great depression.

In order to assist increasing employment it is not unusual for governments to offer considerable inducements for companies to set up operations in an area of high unemployment. The inducements can range from tax breaks through training and building grants through to the provision of infrastructure construction. That governments are keen to assist business in providing economic growth is shown by the fact that according to Klein (2000), the proportion of corporate taxation as a percentage of total federal revenue has dropped from 32% in 1952 to 11.5% in 1998.

Encouraging companies by decreasing taxation presents governments with a dilemma. If corporate taxes fall then how is the shortfall to be made up? Squaring the circle helps – as more people are in work, both the need to spend on welfare decreases and the yield from income taxes should increase. This makes economic sense and provided that wages are sufficient so that they do not need any form of government top-up thus eating into the tax yield, the system may well work. If, however, the inducements are so large that individual taxes have to be increased then a vicious circle can begin. It is no use reducing property taxes for a company to relocate if the community then has to raise personal property taxes to a level that nobody who works at the new factory etc. can afford to live in the area.

The perceived wisdom is that encouraging organizations into an area will rejuvenate the economy and lead to a rise in prosperity for not just the workers at the enterprise but shopkeepers, bus drivers, plumbers, carpenters etc. – all will eventually benefit. Provided that the wages paid are sufficient and that the jobs are permanent, the above is indeed the case. However, where job insecurity still exists and only low wages are paid then general prosperity is less likely to rise and may actually decrease.

In countries like the UK with minimum wage regulations that can and are enforced by the courts this is less likely to happen, but then some companies will not relocate to such a jurisdiction. Relocation itself suggests that unless there is a huge increase in demand leading to extra production it is likely that one areas gain has been another's loss.

Ellwood quotes an *LA Times* report that prior to the formation of NAFTA in 1995, the jeans manufacturer Guess? Inc was producing 97% of its product in Los Angeles. By 1997 this figure was down to 35% with 1000 jobs being lost in LA. The company had relocated mainly to Mexico where it opened five factories. Mexico, also a NAFTA member has a lower average wage rate and as there will be no import restrictions in moving the product into the US, it made economic sense to relocate production to a lower cost area. Corporations are not primarily in the social care business, they are expected to make a profit for their owners – the investors and that means increasing profits. If the price charged cannot be raised then this means cutting costs.

EXPORT PROCESSING ZONES (EPZs)

A considerable amount of the foreign direct investment (FDI) into developing nations has been into operations in export processing zones (EPZs) – areas set up by governments where raw materials are imported and finished products manufactured and exported free of any customs duties. Developed from the freeport concept, EPZs are almost mini-economies of their own. The goods produced vary from clothes to consumer electronics and the advantage for the manufacturer or assembler is that they are able to operate free from many of the custom's restrictions they might face in a more traditional environment. Klein (2000) has profiled the operation of such zones in the Philippines and concludes that the ones she studied operate at very low wage rates combined with harsh working conditions. As Klein points out the EPZs with their modern buildings and well laid out roads and open spaces contrast with the abject poverty of much of the surrounding areas – areas where the workers live. There appears, from Klein's comments, to be little to differentiate the EPZs from a previous generation of sweatshops in terms of wages and working practices.

One of the major issues facing governments promoting EPZs is that of the "swallows." These are companies that move in and take advantage of tax exemptions, grants etc. and then move to another similar area if better inducements are offered. This does nothing for the long-term prosperity of an area or for job security. In fact its effect is very negative as in order to attract another company, even more inducements have to be made and workers may be required to accept even lower wages and longer hours.

CHILD LABOR

It is a sad fact that although slavery was supposed to have been abolished in the nineteenth century, actual slavery still exists in Africa where people are still kidnapped and sold, and to a lesser degree in the employment of child labor for subsistence (or below) wages in many parts of the developing world. There was an outcry in the US when it was discovered that soccer balls were being produced in Asia by very young children and then being sold at a premium in the US market. The United Nations organization and charities such as Save the Children and Christian Aid are making determined efforts to stamp out child labor. As a practice it is counter-productive, for although a child may produce something at a low cost, without education that child is never going to put anything back into society. Unfortunately the illness and mortality rates among child laborers are very high and the human cost of saving a few dollars, pounds, euros, yen etc. is incalculable.

The consumer reaction

Nike, under its charismatic CEO Phil Knight, has been one of the brand successes of the late twentieth and early twenty-first centuries. Nike has outsourced much of its production. Named for the Greek goddess of Victory, Nike's home is in Oregon and is actually the largest employer in Portland, where the company is a leader in local philanthropy. The high quality of Nike's sneakers (called trainers in the UK) and other sportswear products have ensured that the Nike logo the "swoosh" is recognized and respected throughout the world.

Unfortunately in 1997, according to Klein, an anti-Nike movement began in the US based on concerns about outsourcing, low wages paid abroad and child labor. Even school boards were debating whether to accept Nike donations. When Nike stores are picketed and the nation's youth begins to question whether they should purchase products from companies that are outsourcing and thus denying that youth a possible future job – the companies have to listen. No corporation is actually bigger than its customers.

To give Knight his due he has answered his critics and has introduced wage rises in Indonesia where many of the products are manufactured. Klein claims that the poor public relations were in part responsible for some bad financial results in 1998, something Nike had to take seriously.

In the UK a threatened boycott of Shell over their plans for the disposal of the Brent Spar oil platform and its occupation by Greenpeace in a blaze of publicity produced a reversal of policy.

It may be that the global consumer, who rightly wants low prices, may have realized that there is a social cost that can be too high to justify. If that is true, then global corporations are going to have to consider not only their customer's material needs but also their emotional ones.

THE THREAT TO DEMOCRACY

The anti-globalization protesters claim that globalization is a threat to democracy. How can this be, given the size of nations? As was shown earlier in this chapter, many global corporations are bigger than some sovereign nations when measured economically. As they have more resource they can call a louder tune. There have long been theories that governments have fallen due to the efforts of large corporations who stood to benefit from a change in regime. As Ransom (2001) has reported, it has long been believed that it was United Fruit that orchestrated US government support for the overthrow of the elected government of Guatemala in 1954 – a government that was poised to expropriate 400,000 acres of United Fruit banana plantations as part of its support for better wages and conditions. Again, the UK government's role in protecting oil supplies in the Middle East in the 1930s and 40s owed much to strategic military interests but was in no small measure a support mechanism for the UK oil companies.

The key text in this area is David Korten's *When Corporations Rule the World* (1996). It is one of those volumes when science fiction meets current reality and should be read by all involved in global expansion. Even if one disagrees with his contentions about the power of global corporations it provides useful background on the beliefs of those who oppose further globalization.

Anthony Giddens, the director of the London School of Economics, presented the prestigious Reith Lectures (named for Lord Reith the legendary developer of the BBC) in 1999 (published in book form as *Runaway World*). He points out that for many in the developing world, globalization looks very like a Western takeover of their culture and traditions and that organizations need to be much more sensitive to local feelings. This is achievable. The early Christian Church expanded by incorporating the customers of other religions – a process known as transmutation. This is why Christmas is celebrated in the middle of winter (the solstice, an important time in many early religions) rather than in March when scholars believe the nativity actually occurred. If organizations move too quickly to make local culture the same as their home culture this is likely to bring about conflict with traditionalists. The complaints about Western influence by Islamic fundamentalists extend beyond the religious and political to the commercial icons of the west.

Noreena Hertz, writing in *The Silent Takeover* (2001) is concerned that the growth in globalization at a time of declining interest in political activity is leading to greater unaccountability of global corporations. The low turnouts in the US 2000 presidential elections and the 2001 UK general election indicate a disenchantment or, at the least, complacency with the political process. The funding of politics is another issue in the globalization debate. Large corporations in the US can and do fund candidates to a high degree. In the UK political donations are controlled but directorships can be offered and one ex-minister was recently imprisoned for accepting gifts and hospitality from a commercial organization, not declaring it and then seeking to sue a newspaper that reported on the issue. If politics ceases to be "government of the people, by the people and for the people" (President Abraham Lincoln, the Gettysburg Address, November 19, 1863) but just for special interest groups, then the whole foundation of democracy is threatened.

It is doubtful whether there is a global plot for one or more organizations to take over the world. Such a scenario rightly belongs to James Bond, 007 to resolve. However, global corporations have a duty to ensure that what they do, be it in monetary or environmental terms (the issues of the International Monetary Fund and the environmental concerns of the world are beyond the remit of this book but are very important), is not only for the benefit of their investors but for the whole of society – a society that is increasingly global in nature.

ETHICAL INVESTMENTS

That concerns are growing has been demonstrated by the increasing popularity of ethical investment funds. Ethical investors are only prepared to put their money into companies, products and countries they approve of. They may eschew totalitarianism, religious persecution, child labor, exploitation, deforestation, tobacco or alcohol etc. This type of fund is a growing area for financial advisors and companies need to consider how such investors might react to any breach of their values. A flood of stocks onto the market can have a devastating effect on a company's prospects.

BEST PRACTICE
Body Shop/Anita Roddick
Anita Roddick is known all over the world as the founder of the Body Shop. Started in 1976, by 2000 the chain consisted of 1700 stores serving 84 million customers in 24 different languages.

In her business ethic Roddick seeks to be both an environmentalist and a successful businesswomen. The Body Shop's proactive stance on recycling for instances owes as much to a concern about the environment as it does to economic benefits.

Roddick seeks to work with indigenous populations rather than to exploit them. It has not always been easy. Roddick has claimed that Body Shop was virtually unmarketable in the US. The group refuses to use products tested on animals – that stance cut them off from 50% of the raw materials they needed and yet through perseverance the message has been accepted. She states that she was much influenced by the US champion of the consumer, Ralph Nader, and his faith in citizen power.

Body Shop is a small organization when considered alongside the global giants, yet it has shown that companies can succeed by working in partnership not only with the workforce but with nature itself and that as environmental awareness grows this may be the way forward for all industries.

Roddick's story is contained in her autobiography, *Business as Usual*, an entertaining read and a good insight into one of the latter twentieth-century's business visionaries.

KEY LEARNING POINTS

» Many see globalization as Westernization.
» Global organizations have responsibilities to more than just their investors.
» No organization is bigger than its customers.
» The anti-globalization lobby believes that there is a moral and social dimension to business.

The State of the Art of Going Global

Companies that wish to expand globally need to consider the following points:

- » Where to expand to.
- » How to ensure that they will be welcomed.
- » Whether they will expand overtly in their own name or covertly by acquiring local companies. They need to remember that local companies and brands may have a loyal customer base that can be retained.
- » The four elements to going global are:
  1. The culture
  2. The actual product/service
  3. The staff people
  4. Competition from other global and local players.
- » Staff should be treated with equity across the company even if equality is not possible.
- » High price differentials for the same product in different areas can lead to parallel importing.
- » Pseudo expansion is the use of EPZs etc. to establish a low-cost manufacturing operation without trying to compete in the local market.

If the previous chapter presented a rather negative side to the concept of globalization, this chapter is designed to redress the balance. While there are organizations to whom the idea of globalization is just another means of cutting costs, there are many others whose strategy is to offer products and services on a global basis and to use the breaking down of trade barriers to achieve this objective. It is these organizations whose trade names have become part of the global lexicon: McDonald's, Black and Decker, BMW, Ford, many of the sportswear manufacturers, cosmetic producers, even those in staple products, Nestlé, Mars and, of course Coca-Cola and Pepsi Cola.

WHERE TO GO GLOBAL?

Organizations do not usually expand in a haphazard manner. They undertake careful research to ensure that there is a market for them, that they will be welcomed in that market and that the expansion will not cause problems elsewhere.

In the previous chapter the tax advantages offered to relocating organizations were mentioned and any financial assistance is normally very welcome. There have been instances where organizations have not been welcomed in other areas. China once placed a two-year ban on Disney films as a result of Disney releasing *Kundun*, a film about the Dali Lama, although most countries are only too pleased to welcome foreign investment.

Home base countries may place restrictions on expansion. There have been a number of attempts to start a Florida–Havana ferry service, all of which have fallen foul of the US government. It is not possible to import Cuban cigars into the US on a legal basis. The UK and other countries had long-time bans on their companies trading with South Africa until apartheid was lifted and it is not unusual for arms sales to be blocked if the home country feels that they may threaten its foreign policy. Needless to say there appear to be many cases of these restrictions being circumvented.

On a local basis there may be objections to "foreign infiltration" especially if it provides competition to indigenous organizations or threatens local culture. Fundamental Islamic regimes have tried to ban Western goods that they feel are likely to infringe moral or cultural values.

The City of Canterbury in the southeast of England (the Cathedral contains the tomb of Thomas Becket while the Archbishop of Canterbury is the head of the global Anglican/Episcopalian Christian Community) is a town of old buildings in its center and while not refusing permission for McDonald's to operate, did insist that the "M arches" symbol be much less prominent than is normally the case.

In the US, some school boards have tried to ban the availability of the best-selling Harry Potter books for children on the grounds that they are about witchcraft and offend religious sensibilities.

OVERT, COVERT, AND PSEUDO GLOBAL EXPANSION

Companies can expand globally either overtly or covertly. An overt expansion occurs when customers and suppliers are made immediately aware that there has been a change and that a new player has entered the market either by starting a completely new operation or by purchasing an existing player and changing to the new name and brands. The covert approach is to acquire an existing player but to change very little so that it may not be apparent that a new company has entered the market. There may well be very important commercial reasons for acting in this way. Brand names can have considerable loyalty and changing them may mean the loss of a loyal customer base. P&O, a UK company that is the subject of a case study in Chapter 7, wanted to re-enter the rapidly expanding US cruise market in 1974. P&O had attempted to enter the US market earlier but the name, very familiar in the UK was relatively unknown to US vacation and cruise seekers. P&O acquired Princess Cruises, a US company that had built up a loyal customer base since its foundation in 1965. P&O kept the name of the company and the name of the ships. Princess Cruises became one of the major players under the P&O houseflag but it was some time before the P&O lettering appeared on the sides of the ships. There was no reason for US customers to know that their vacation was actually with a UK company. They dealt with the Princess Cruises office in Santa Monica (Los Angeles), the currency on board was the US dollar, the entertainment and food were geared to US tastes and the funnel carried the original Princess symbol. At the same time P&O ran their traditional parallel cruise operation for the UK market. As time has gone by the P&O component of Princess has become much more visible as customers have become used to the idea of multi-national, global operations.

As will be mentioned below, General Motors kept the old Rootes Group brand names such as Vauxhall when they expanded into the UK market. Ford has always been overt about their expansion in the main stream market but less so in the luxury end – the Jaguar brand has still been kept. Sports goods suppliers such as Nike, Adidas etc. have also been quite overt, the more well known a brand is globally, the easier is overt expansion – indeed customers may be clamoring for the chance to acquire the product locally.

The process of moving manufacturing into Export Processing Zones (EPZs), covered in the previous chapter, may often be a case of pseudo global expansion as the company is not attempting to move into a new market for sales but just to cut manufacturing costs. It is a sad reflection on globalization that many quite mundane products could not be afforded by those who produce them and who thus do not form part of the potential market for the product.

In developing a strategy for going global, there are four key elements, the first is the product/service itself, the second is the people who are to manufacture/sell/deliver the product or service and these are both "surrounded" by the third factor, the culture of the area in question and of the organization, a point considered in the next section. Finally, there is the question of competition, both indigenous and from others seeking to expand their markets.

CULTURE

Culture is considered in detail in the *ExpressExec* book *Managing Diversity*. Culture can be defined as the "way we do things around here" and differs from place to place across the globe, between ethnic groups and between organizations. There is, fortunately, a wealth of material on managing cultural differences and the reader is advised to consult *Managing Diversity* (Chapters 5 and 6) in this Series, *Riding the Waves of Culture* (1993) by Fons Trompenaars, *When Cultures Collide* (2000) by Richard D Lewis and *Managing Cultural Differences* (2000) by Philip Harris and Robert Morgan (details of these texts are given in Chapter 9).

It would be a foolish organization that did not take account of the culture in which it was planning to operate. Different cultures have different attitudes to achievement, the application of rules, gender, time etc. all of which Trompenaars has considered in depth.

There is a whole range of cultural issues that an organization needs to consider if expansion into another area of the world is being proposed. These include:

» what form of hierarchies does the culture encourage
» attitudes to gender
» attitudes to age and experience
» who makes buying decisions
» what is acceptable and not acceptable in advertising copy
» employment rights and legislation
» business practices that may run counter to those in the organization's home country.

It may well be that some of the above run counter to the organization's own beliefs and culture. Most organizations based in developed countries have policy relating to equal opportunities; this is not always the case elsewhere. The organization, by being sensitive, can perhaps use their policies to encourage change and enlightenment. Bribery is against the law in most developed countries, whereas in some parts of the world "commissions" is the expected way of doing business. More than one CEO has fallen foul of this in doing business the local way and then being criticized and punished at home. As Eddy *et al.* (1976) reported, Dan Haughton, CEO of Lockheed and the company's president, Carl Kotchian, were forced to resign in February 1976 (Friday 13th, of all days) as a result of questionable payments to, amongst others, Dutch and Japanese government officials during the sales campaigns for the Lockheed F-104 Starfighter and the L-1011 Tri-Star jet airliner.

Advertising can also be another area where culture clashes can occur. In the early days of television a number of US companies who also operated in the UK tried to import US advertisements directly onto UK screens only to find out that although the language used might be similar, UK cultural tastes were different to those in the US. Since then there have been examples of advertisements that have been truly global in nature but they have been few and far between. Nike, the

British Airways "Global" advertisement featuring people from all over the world making a globe and the famous "I'd like to buy the world a Coke" advertisements worked almost everywhere. Others often need to be customized for the particular culture.

Even throughout the English-speaking world there are considerable cultural and subtle linguistic differences. The concept that the US and the UK are "divided by a common language" is very apt. Christopher Davies (1997) has provided a useful guide as to how the British can avoid making mistakes in the US, and visa versa, in *Divided by a Common Language* – a humorous but useful text for those who live on one English-speaking side of the Atlantic and are working or vacationing on the other.

It is not difficult to discover the cultural norms of an area and it is nearly always worth taking the time to do so. Suppliers, customers and employees will always be happier with an organization and products or services that they feel comfortable with, and the more in tune the organization and what it offers is with cultural norms, the more comfortable people will be and thus the more likely they are to give their business to the organization.

Products/services

It has already been mentioned in this material that the same types of products and services are now available on a global basis. However, as George S. Yip points out in *Total Global Strategy* (1992), the idea of a completely similar product/service available all over the globe is a myth. There are nearly always local variations as a result of differences and culture.

At the simplest level these may be purely linguistic. Coca-Cola is one of the most standardized global products but even Coke labels need to reflect the language of the user. It is noticeable that many products now include multi-lingual labels and instruction. Even mundane products such as shower gel on sale in the UK may include labels with English, French, Portuguese, Italian etc. lettering on the same label in an attempt to cut costs. Some nations prefer certain colors to others and if this can be accommodated in production costs, all well and good. It shows that the organization has actually been considering the preferences of its customers.

It is vitally important that effective market research is carried out to see whether changes need to be made to a standard product. There may well be legislative reasons for doing so. While automobiles now look very similar in most countries, governments have different safety and emission regulations and these need to be catered for. Not all countries drive on the right-hand side of the road. The UK, Eire, India and Pakistan, Cyprus, Australia, New Zealand and one part of the US still drive on the left. (The answer to which part of the US still drives on the left is the US Virgin Islands. At the time they were acquired from Denmark, Scandinavia still drove on the left). Modern manufacturing techniques have made it easier to produce left- and right-hand drive automobiles using the same jigs, machine tools and production lines but the issue also affects headlight lens for example – small points but very important ones. The introduction of the Chrysler Neon into the UK after the Daimler – Chrysler merger showed how these issues need to be thought about. The position of the clock on the radio is such that while it is clearly visible on the left-hand drive version, in the UK right-hand drive model it is obscured by the driver's left arm. A small point but still an irritating one, especially as the car is such good value for money in the UK.

There may be demographic differences. A product that is dominated by female sales in one culture may be more male oriented in another. Small automobiles are a good example. Something that appeals to youth in one place may be initially more attractive to an older age range in another. The mobile telephone market usually starts with the older business sector as the main purchasers, with youth following on. The organization must examine such factors so as to decide where to pitch its entry. As a market becomes more mature then it will bring along those who have grown up with the product. In the 1960s, Coca-Cola etc. were youth drinks. That generation has grown up but still drinks those brands when buying sodas.

McDonald's have become famous for both a highly standardized product and a highly standardized level of service and delivery, but even they make local adaptations: Islamic and Jewish cultures do not eat pork; the French expect alcohol to be served in such establishments while people in the UK do not. Within the standardized product, McDonald's have been able to cater for local variations. The knowledge that such variations are necessary at the outset of an expansion can greatly aid in building a loyal customer base.

It may be necessary to change the name of a product to suit local preferences although the current trend is to adapt names that are culturally neutral. Many of the automobile producers actually make names up, the Ford Ka and the Citroen Saxo being examples, or use numbers or a word that is clearly recognized globally, Mondeo, Neon etc. The UK brand name of the confectionery Snickers was, for a long time Marathon until it was realized that UK purchasers would accept Snickers. Organizations need to be very careful that what is acceptable in one language is not unacceptable in another.

Even if the product stays the same, the packaging may change to reflect local culture. Pictures of Caucasian children on a product destined for Asia would be insensitive. US and UK cornflakes taste the same and the packaging is similar but not quite the same. Kellogg's have managed to achieve what Coca-Cola has – many in the UK think that Kellogg's Cornflakes are a UK product. Perhaps the true indicator of having "gone global" is that people in a particular market believe that the product/service/brand is indigenous to that market. There are people in the US who truly believe that Shell is a US firm and those in the UK who believe that it is British – it is actually Royal Dutch Shell.

According to Yip (see Chapters 8 and 9), there are only 19 truly global brands, the top five of which are: Coca-Cola, Sony, Mercedes Benz, Kodak, and Disney. Apparently nearly everybody in the world knows about and recognizes these names. Not surprisingly Levi-Strauss, Kellogg's and Ford are also in the list.

Services are one type of economic good that often requires considerable variation. Financial services including banking, insurance, investments and pensions are subject to considerable national legislation. The major financial institutions such as HSBC (Hong Kong and Shanghai Banking Corporation) overcome the problem by acquiring local operators and in many cases keeping the original brand names but adapting their services to fit corporate guidelines.

Pricing

In the next section the issue of remuneration will be considered and the problem of whether to pay global or national rates. A similar issue occurs with pricing. As standards of living differ across the world and wages may be higher or lower it should be expected that costs will also differ and thus the price charged. As people become more and more mobile, however, they are likely to come across these price differentials. It is already less expensive for UK motorists to order and pay for a new vehicle elsewhere in Europe as UK prices have traditionally been higher – the EU are currently taking steps to harmonize prices to a greater degree. Seeing something for sale for less elsewhere might lead to customer dissatisfaction and also to the problem of parallel importing.

Parallel importing

In the 1990s, many companies became concerned about the phenomenon of parallel importing. This was an issue that affected, amongst others, the pharmaceutical and the music industries as a result of the lowering of trade barriers especially within the European Union.

Many of the concerned manufacturers had been accused of price fixing in the UK by supermarkets and discount retailers who had been unable to obtain supplies directly to sell at a discount. The manufacturers, it was claimed, wished to keep prices at a higher level in the UK than elsewhere (see above).

The prices of many products fluctuate according to supply and demand and may be relatively lower in one country than another – for example, the price of books and compact discs in the US compared to the UK.

The supermarkets and discount retailers have dealt with this problem by buying supplies from abroad at local wholesale prices, re-importing them into the UK and selling at a discount. This is a practice known as parallel importing and is a direct consequence of going global and the price differentials that are bound to occur.

In 2001 the UK supermarket giant, Tesco, and the US jeans manufacturer, Levi-Strauss, became embroiled in a legal argument when the latter tried to stop Tesco selling their product at discounted prices. Tesco were importing the jeans using parallel import methods much to the chagrin of the manufacturer whose regular retailers were charging a much higher price.

Manufacturers claim that the specifications may be different and that this accounts for the differences in price – claims that are currently under investigation by the Competition Commission in the UK. Levi-Strauss also claimed that they provided considerable support and training etc. to their regular suppliers and thus incurred higher costs.

PEOPLE

Managing Diversity, companion material in the *ExpressExec* series, contains details of the management of people across cultural boundaries and the point is made that diversity is something to be celebrated and not a problem.

Companies expanding globally will have to take account of the different employment practices that may be present in the areas they move into. While large economic blocs such as the EU are harmonizing employment rights, practices, and legislation, there are still considerable differences throughout the globe. Pat Joynt and Bob Morton have edited a useful volume, *The Global HR Manager* (1999), that considers the issues that face those responsible for the human resource management (HRM)/personnel function in organizations operating on a global stage. They have introduced what they call "the Seven Cs" of international HRM:

» Competition
» Culture
» Communications
» Competencies
» Compensation
» Careers
» Collaboration.

Competition

To Joynt and Morton, competition (the subject of the final section in this chapter) is concerned with ensuring that the overall strategy of the company is correct. It is important that the company knows what its core and non-core activities are, and what can and cannot be localized. As Peters and Waterman stated in *In Search of Excellence* (1982), productivity and success comes from the people within an organization and thus competitiveness, while partially dependent on price and quality is also affected by the caliber of personnel.

Culture

The importance of culture has already been stressed in this chapter. Culture is a function of the people in a society and thus HRM has to occur within the dominant culture. It is no use trying to impose work patterns and ethics from one culture to another and to expect instant success. It takes time for people to become accustomed to new ways of doing things. There are also other cultural aspects to be taken into account. Religion – do staff need prayer breaks, the position of women; how can equality be practiced in a culture that relegates women to second place?; hierarchies – can all the staff eat together in a culture where people are very caste conscious? These are all HRM issues that need to be thought through and, if necessary compromises agreed that allow all parties to retain their integrity.

Communications

It is not only managers who can use the new communication technologies to pass information to each other. It is possible to ensure that all employees are part of a network. The importance of the communication network was shown by the Boeing case study in Chapter 4. One potential downside is that as employees across the globe find it easier to communicate with each other, they will also find out about any differences in employment practices at different sites. While there may be excellent reasons for these, it does not follow that staff will always understand or agree with different treatment.

Competencies

One of the things that remains fairly constant wherever a company operates is the core competencies of staff. Training can often be arranged on a global or regional basis and this can provide a useful opportunity for bringing staff together. Before its merger with Norwich Union, the insurance company, General Accident ran a management program at its headquarters outside the Scottish town of Perth to which staff from all over the globe were brought to work together. In order to assist the local economy the company also made a limited number of places available to local colleges etc. for their staff to gain an understanding of the insurance industry in general and a local employer in particular. Even if a global training program is impracticable, regional events can be used to both train and network. It is vital that staff members have the same level of competence wherever they work for the company.

Compensation

As covered earlier, wage rates tend to be determined by local conditions. A company moving into a new area has to ensure that it pays enough to gain high quality staff but not so much as to upset the local economic balance. The movement into low wage economies was covered in the previous chapter and this has been a recent trend. Low wage is relative, however, and a company in a low wage economy that pays a little more than others may manage to poach all the best staff. In the developed world there are particular minimum wage requirements, holiday, sickness, maternity benefits that must be factored in and obeyed.

Careers

If a company moves into an area by acquisition it will acquire the staff of the original company. There may well be legislation in place protecting their position for the immediate future. The company would be wise if it bore in mind their sensitivity to their career path. Many will have been working their way upwards and any new structures need to be put in place sensitively if the motivation of such people is to be maintained. While becoming part of a global operation may seem like a threat, there is also the opportunity for staff to move to other parts of the world as part of their career experience.

Collaboration

Going global requires collaboration between all levels of management. Dealing as they are with the rights etc. of the work force, human resource managers need to keep in constant touch with their colleagues to ensure equity throughout the company. Equality – i.e. treating everybody the same – is probably impossible in a global operation but equity – treating people in a similar way contingent upon the local circumstances – is possible and should be the aim of every global organization.

When a machine breaks down it can be repaired. When a person breaks down it is not so easy. People are the biggest resource any organization possesses and thus need to be treated properly if they are to give of their best. It is people who add value.

COMPETITION

It is rare for a company to move into a completely virgin market. There are already likely to be a set of players in that market competing with each other.

The company coming in should be aware that competition among existing players might well be paused in order to see off a new threat. While the WTO and many governments preach about a free market, governments can and do place obstacles in the way of outsiders by using preferences or tariff barriers. While the company can often take legal action to remove these barriers this can take time and thus there is the opportunity cost of lost business. The wise company planning to go global analyses the situation very carefully before making a move.

KEY LEARNING POINTS

» People are the most important resource any organization possesses and should be treated with equity.
» Existing competition may be paused to fight off entry by a new
player.
» Different areas have different employment etc. legislation and
this must be taken into account when developing policies.
» High price differentials can cause the company problems as they
encourage retailers etc. to practice parallel importing.
» Acquiring an existing organization is a useful way into a market
and can bring with it a loyal customer base.

Going Global Success Stories

Companies from the US, Europe and Asia that have made a success of going into the global marketplace:

- » Amazon.com
- » P&O
- » Sony
- » Timeline and key inserts to accompany each case study.

The three case studies presented in this chapter represent not only three successful global companies headquartered in different parts of the world but also three very different typologies – the first an old product sold in a brand new way, the second an old-established company in a seemingly traditional industry and the third, a new(ish) company selling the products of the latest technology. What links the three is their success in going global.

AMAZON.COM

Globally, Amazon.com is probably one of the best-known names of the new dot com companies that seemed to spring up (and sometimes disappear just as quickly) at the end of the 1990s and into the early years of the new century.

The founder of Amazon.com, ex-Princeton graduate Jeff Bezos, is the son of a Cuban immigrant to the US. Bezos' first job (on his vacation while still a student) was as a programmer/analyst for his father's company, the oil giant Exxon, actually in Norway where his father was based at the time.

On leaving Princeton, Bezos became involved with the computer side of the banking industry and began to see the potential of the Internet for commerce. It is now generally agreed that the birth of the World Wide Web was in 1993 (Spector, 2000) but even before that the proactive were registering their names. Among them were a very small number of booksellers, the first being Computer Literacy. Research that Bezos carried out for his then employer in 1994 showed that Internet usage was growing at an incredible 2,300% per annum. Bezos decided to consider exactly which products/services would be best to offer, using the Internet as the supplier customer interface. His choices included software, clothing, and books, and it became apparent from his research that books, a product going back centuries, were a very good choice for the most up-to-date medium of trade.

The book trade has always been fragmentary with a large number of publishers in different countries together with retail outlets ranging from small, independent, one-site operations to national and, latterly, international chains. Spector (2000) reports that in the US even the largest of the publishers, Random House had less than 10% of the market and that the two largest retail chains, Barnes and Noble, and

Borders (who also have a large UK operation) accounted for less than 25% of the $30bn of adult sales in 1994.

Bookselling is big business, however, as reading is a popular activity – in 1996 global book sales netted $82bn. In the UK the 1990s saw a deregulation within the industry with the scrapping of the net book agreement that had fixed prices. Booksellers could now discount their prices and the major chains did just that, with "three for two" deals etc. on novels becoming increasingly common. In the US this trend had been led by Crown Books in the 1980s.

The major problem that traditional bookstores have is the need for space for selling and warehousing. Even the largest store in the US or UK could only carry a small percentage of the 1.5 million English language books in print at any one time. Bezos realized that a virtual bookstore using the Internet could place no limit on the number of titles available to the customer. His operation could acquire stock direct from the publishers or from one of the small number of book distributors. The Internet technology would make the customer's task of searching for a title relatively simple and a check could be kept on customer preferences so that recommendations could be made, thus personalizing the service to the same level as possible when using a small independent book store on a regular basis. There, it is the owner who knows the customer; in the Bezos vision it is the computer.

Moving to Seattle, Bezos spent much of 1994 meeting people and learning about the book business. As has been stressed in this material, he conducted a thorough analysis of the market and the competition.

In November 1994, Bezos and his associates began the Amazon.com operation in a converted garage in a section of Seattle. Using the database of "books in print" and information from the Library of Congress (look at the front of nearly any book in the English language that is likely to reach the US or UK markets and you will find Library of Congress and The British Library statements that the book is included in their catalogs).

The company was launched to the public in 1995 by which time it had acquired a database of more than one million titles. An ordering system, customer identification system, distribution, and the all important credit card facilities had been established. No longer need those with access to the Internet (a growing percentage of the US population) travel to a bookstore. No matter how remote they were, they could browse the book lists online and order with confidence. The only thing they could not do was to scan the shelves and the pages of the books on them. However, more and more information about content is available in the media, on the Internet and on the Amazon.com site itself.

From the beginning, Amazon.com discounted their best sellers by 10% with some titles discounted by up to 30%. The writer of this material lives in the North of Scotland and has found over a period of using Amazon.co.uk (the UK arm – see later) that the discount offered usually wipes out the postage costs. As the nearest conventional bookshop is 20 miles away from him with the larger shops being about 50 miles distant; a considerable time and financial saving is made by ordering online. For this case study, it is possible for the writer to state with confidence that the way the Amazon.com site works does provide a degree of a personal relationship, and that entering the site (provided the "cookie" has not been deleted from the PC) elicits a personal welcome back and news of the latest releases in the customer's particular areas of interest based on previous purchasing patterns.

Like the vast majority of the early dot com operations Bezos lost money – $303,000 in 1995. However even so early on in the history of the company over 2,000 people per day were visiting the site and within two years this would increase to 80,000.

By 1996 Bezos had acquired sufficient venture capital to expand the Amazon.com operation and the company had increased to 150 employees and more importantly, $16m in sales – prompting an approach from the major bookseller, Barnes and Noble, although no deal materialized. Also in that year an associates program was launched whereby the owners of other web sites could direct their visitors to Amazon.com and receive a small payment if this resulted in a purchase.

In 1997, Amazon.com made its initial public offering (IPO). Despite the fact that the company was still losing money, £3m in the first quarter of 1997, sales had boomed and investors considered Amazon.com worth buying and the IPO was oversubscribed. The opening price was $18 and after an initial rise and fall ended the year at $52 – not bad for a company that had only made losses.

Global expansion

In 1998 Bezos began talks with Bertelsmann AG, the Germany media giant that already had a small bookselling operation, BOL. This led to nothing for Amazon.com but Bertelsmann later acquired 50% of the Barnes and Noble online operation – competition was growing. Amazon then acquired a UK online operation and a smaller online bookshop in Germany. This gave Bezos an entry into the lucrative UK and German markets. The UK was important, as London is a large publishing center for English language books. Most of the major publishers operate parallel UK (often London) and US (New York or Cambridge MA) operations.

These moves led to the formation of Amazon.co.uk in the UK and Amazon.co.de in Germany. As has been stated in this material the addition of a local country web designator – .uk and .de – gives the customer the feeling that they are dealing with a national supplier and not a foreign interloper. Another small example of this is that the customer loads their purchases onto a shopping cart on Amazon.com but into a shopping basket on Amazon.co.uk, where US published and supplied books are dual priced in dollars and pounds sterling.

This expansion has led to certain copyright problems. US copyright law bars the importation of copyrighted books for commercial resale (but not for private use). Bezos considered that a US citizen buying from Amazon.co.uk (easily accessed from the US) was just the same as flying to London, buying the book and bringing it back to the US. This argument is still underway. Certainly users of Amazon.co.uk have no difficulty in acquiring US books through the site, as the writer can testify.

The decision to expand into the UK and Germany was sensible as much of the British Commonwealth will happily buy from the UK and central Europeans are accustomed to doing business with German companies. With its local distribution systems, Amazon.co.uk and its German counterpart have grown rapidly to become an established part of the local book-buying scene.

By 1999, Amazon as a group had expanded into CD and DVD sales through its online Zshops and in 2001 started to sell electronic items including cameras. In 1999 total sales were $2.6bn, and in 2001 Amazon acquired the Borders online operation.

By 2001 the global expansion had included two further very important markets – France and Japan. Where next? China, India – both with large populations and avid readers?

There is no doubt that despite the problems of the dot com companies and the time it takes to move into profit, Bezos has provided the world with an effective means of buying an old product – the humble book – as important today as it has been throughout history for the transmission of knowledge, culture and ideas and for providing sheer pleasure through reading.

Fig. 7.1 shows a time line for Amazon.

AMAZON.COM – KEY INSIGHTS

» In depth analysis of market and competition conducted before operations commenced
» Systems in place before operations started
» Offered a new way of doing something – a way that added value
» Expansion into two European markets with a tradition of high book sales
» Sites reflect local preferences
» Customer feels like an individual
» Further expansion into other high literacy areas.

P&O

Amazon.com, the subject of the previous case study is a new organization engaged in an old activity – book selling but using a brand new method of reaching customers on a global basis. Sony, the third of the case studies, is a relatively new organization offering a range of products that are technologically very recent. P&O – or the Peninsular and Oriental Steam Navigation Company to use the full title – is an old organization that has adapted to the global marketplace and survived and flourished in competitive areas; something many of its original competitors have been unable to do.

P&O is an old established UK company having been founded as the Peninsular Steam Navigation Company in 1837 to serve Spain and Portugal (the Iberian Peninsular countries) from UK ports. Even

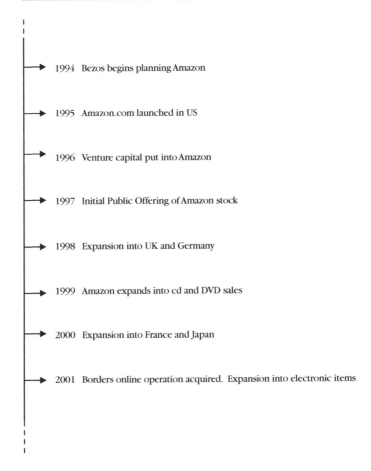

1994 Bezos begins planning Amazon

1995 Amazon.com launched in US

1996 Venture capital put into Amazon

1997 Initial Public Offering of Amazon stock

1998 Expansion into UK and Germany

1999 Amazon expands into cd and DVD sales

2000 Expansion into France and Japan

2001 Borders online operation acquired. Expansion into electronic items

Fig. 7.1 Amazon.com time line.

today the P&O house flag/corporate logo is based on the colors of the royal houses of Spain and Portugal. Today they operate cruise ships (as a separate company, as described later), container and bulk cargo ships, passenger and freight ferries, river cruises, Rhine barges, road transport and holidays on a global basis. Until recently P&O controlled the building concern of Bovis, responsible for the restoration of the Statue of Liberty in New York Harbor and even owned the prestigious exhibition centers of Olympia and Earls Court in London.

Despite losses in both world wars, the P&O shipping operation grew to cover the world, with the exception of the North and South Atlantic routes. From the Iberian Peninsular the line company extended its operations to India then China and Australia and finally from Asia to Vancouver. Up to the present day P&O has operated over 500 ships, and in the words of David L Williams (1998) writing about P&O, "Larger and more luxuriously appointed ships were to be progressively introduced offering an unparalleled breadth of service and frequency of sailings. With 50 years the P&O was to become, in the public mind, synonymous with ocean travel."

The large shipping companies have always been international in operation but, as was shown in Chapter 3 when considering the activities of J P Morgan, the governments of maritime nations have also considered them as part of their strategic reserve to be used in time of conflict in the nation's military interests. As late as 1982 P&O were supplying ships including their flagship, the liner *Canberra* for service in the Falkland's conflict of that year. *Canberra* accompanied the landing forces all the way to San Carlos water where the troops went ashore, and it is only by luck that she escaped being damaged.

P&O is interesting as a case study as it is one of the few companies that managed to survive the decimation of the liner trade by the jet airliner and to emerge as strong as ever as a global player.

As a company P&O has always expanded both overtly and covertly (see Chapter 6). Overtly they have undertaken massive building programs for the P&O brand but covertly over the years the company acquired British India, Union Steamship Company of New Zealand, The New Zealand Shipping Company, Federal Steam, Hain Line, Nourse Line, General Steam, Khedivial Mail Line, a majority stake in Orient Line (the original Orient Line, not the current company that is part of Norwegian Cruise Line that is in turn owned byStar Cruises), whose operations and name were completely merged with P&O in 1965, Princess Cruises (as already noted earlier in this material), Sitmar (taken over by Princess in 1988), Aida Cruises in Germany in 2000 and a failed bid for Festival Cruises also in 2000.

In addition there has been the Bovis operation, joint ventures with Nedlloyd, the container ship operation, the acquisition of North of Scotland Ferries and the Townsend Thorensen Ferry operation, and the conference and exhibition centers in London.

By 2001 the P&O Group was concentrating on its original core shipping business operating the following brands:

» P&O Ports
» P&O Scottish Ferries
» P&O North Sea Ferries
» P&O Irish Sea Ferries
» P&O Stena Line (ferry operations across the English Channel)
» P&O Trans European (unit load/container trucking operation)
» P&O Cold Logistics (refrigerated transport and storage)
» P&O Nedlloyd (container ship operations globally)
» P&O Australia (includes P&O Australian Resorts, P&O Maritime Services – ship agency, chartering, tugs etc., P&O Polar Australia – operating polar services for the Australian government)
» Port of Larne (Northern Ireland)
» P&O Princess Cruises (as a separate company, see below for details).

The rest of this case study will concentrate on the cruise operations that, since the demerger in 2000, operates as a completely separate company under the name of P&O Princess Cruises, and will show how a traditional company can expand globally and meet local demand and maintain a high quality of service.

P&O itself was the subject of a takeover attempt by Cunard in the 1980s.

The cruise operation

P&O commenced operations in the cruise sector as early as 1881 but prior to the 1960s, cruising was always a supplement to the main business, which was the liner trade from the UK to the India, Asia and Australasia. The advent of intercontinental passenger jet aircraft decimated the liner trade rapidly, with large numbers of ships being either scrapped or converted to cruising. This occurred at the same time as the UK government imposed currency exchange restrictions, making a foreign vacation almost impossible unless it was to a sterling area. British registered ships were, however, a sterling area and there was a boom in the 1960s of inexpensive cruises out of UK ports on UK flagged vessels of which P&O had a surplus.

At the same time US vacationers were discovering the joys of a Caribbean cruise and the number of companies operating for the US cruise market grew rapidly. Once the UK currency restrictions were lifted Mediterranean package holidays gained in popularity and the UK cruise market diminished to the extent that even P&O were reduced to two ships in the market until the middle of the 1990s when cruising again became popular for UK customers. In 1992, 4.25 million US citizens took a cruise, but by 1999 this was up to 6.25 million. In the UK the 1992 figure was 225,000 but by 1999 had increased three-fold to nearly 750,000. P&O's first incursion into the US market was in the late 1960s with a couple of older ships and the new *Spirit of London* operating under the P&O name. More success came later with the acquisition of the US cruise operator, Princess; the brand name being retained as mentioned earlier.

Local differences

Robert Tillberg, the renowned cruise ship designer, has commented on the difference in the behavior of US and UK cruise customers. The US customers generally require a more hotel type vacation but at sea with frequent port calls. They prefer larger passenger spaces and of course US style entertainment and cuisine. UK cruisers seem to enjoy days at sea and ships with smaller more intimate spaces. It is noteworthy that the traditional UK cruisers tend to talk about decks and cabins while those from the US refer to floors and staterooms.

P&O has been very adept at designing ships for the particular market. While recent years have seen a convergence of taste it is obvious to even an untrained eye that the *Royal Princess*, despite her UK registry, is a floating piece of the US and that the *Oriana* and *Aurora* are British. All the ships are fitted out to a high standard and the service is consistently good, but the US and UK products feel different. Even ships that have been transferred from one market to another undergo expensive refits to make them compatible with the culture of the majority of customers even to the extent of changing the onboard art work.

The expansion into the Australian and German markets has been undertaken in a similar manner. German brand names and ambience have been retained, as the P&O name is not that well known in Germany. In Australia this is less of a problem as P&O has served Australia for many years.

Global operations

The global cruise operations of P&O Princess Cruises are truly that, comprising operations for four different global markets – US, UK, Germany and Australia – plus a niche within the culture marker using a special ship, the *Minerva,* to operate cruises where the emphasis is on culture and history rather than sun, sightseeing and entertainment.

P&O Princess Cruises plc (public limited company) is the third largest cruise company in the world in revenue terms. P&O Princess Cruises was demerged from the main P&O Group in 2000 and floated on the New York and London Stock Exchanges as a separate company, although still using the P&O logo and name. The companies have separate boards. The demerger reflected the growing strength of the cruise sector. P&O Princes Cruises includes, as its functional components, Princess Cruises – the North American premium brand; P&O Cruises, the UK's largest and oldest premium cruise brand; Aida Cruises, one of Germany's fastest growing cruise companies; P&O Cruises (Australia) – a single ship operation; and Swan Hellenic, operating the *Minerva* (see above) in the UK, and *Seetours* in Germany. The company provides premium cruises to Alaska, Northern Europe, the Mediterranean, the Panama Canal, and the Caribbean. The current fleet of 18 ships offering 27,360 berths is set to grow over the next three years with the addition of 8 ships offering a further 17,020 berths.

Headquartered in London, the company employs about 19,000 employees worldwide. In 2000, P&O Princess Cruises carried over 900,000 passengers generating revenue of over $2bn.

As described by Cartwright and Baird (1999) the cruise sector of the vacation industry is one of the fastest growing travel segments, driven by increased disposable income and demographic trends worldwide. P&O Princess's focus for future growth is to build on its strong local brands (see Chapter 6), sustain the high quality of both its ships and service standards, and to increase its global presence.

P&O Princess Cruises' strategy

As a leader in the global cruise industry with products and brands tailored to local markets, P&O Princess's strategy is to:

» *Build on its strengths in the North American cruise sector.* Princess Cruises is one of the strongest cruise brands in North America as a result of its early entry into the market in the 1960s prior to its acquisition by P&O as described earlier. Princess is one of the leading providers of cruises to Alaska (where the company also has a land tours operation), Europe, the Panama Canal and other exotic locations (principally South America, Africa, the South Pacific, the Orient and India).

The intention of the company is to continue to innovate and differentiate the Princess product. The launch of the *Grand Princess* of 109,000 GRT (gross registered tonnes) in 1998 provided the company with the largest passenger ship in the history of sea transportation and a sister, *Golden Princess*, came out in 2001. Such is the fast-growing nature of the cruise industry, however, that these vessels have been somewhat eclipsed by Royal Caribbean's *Eagle Class*, of 137,000 GRT the first of which, *Voyager of the Seas*, came out in 1999. However, Douglas Ward (2001), who compiles the *Berlitz Guide to Cruising and Cruise Ships* on an annual basis, rates the *Grand Princess* as a premium product and the *Voyager of the Seas* as a standard one, suggesting that the Princess product is more upmarket even if the ships are a little smaller. Interestingly, the Princess brand does not seek to be one of the largest operators in the Caribbean, preferring a balance of cruising areas.

Other companies in the sector, especially Carnival, the largest operator in the industry, have a massive presence in the Caribbean. Princess Cruises believe that the introduction of a series of new ships will allow them to compete effectively especially as they are enhancing the level of choice for the customer through new developments such as true restaurant style (''Personal Choice'') dining instead of set sittings which is currently being rolled out to more and more ships within the fleet.

» *Capitalize on the global growth of cruising.* P&O Princess Cruises has leading positions in two of the largest vacation markets outside

North America – the United Kingdom and Germany. P&O Princess Cruises tailors its products to the tastes and preferences of local consumers. The importance of developing brands that appeal to local preferences within the overall quality standards of the organization was covered in Chapter 6 and earlier in this chapter when discussing the difference between US and UK customers in the cruise industry. P&O Cruises and Aida are two of the strongest cruise brands in the UK and Germany respectively and have well-established distribution networks and significant customer bases with high levels of repeat business.

The company plan to strengthen its presence in the UK and Germany through introducing new ships and redeploying ships from the existing Princess fleet. Two Princess ships will be transferred to Germany in Spring 2002 where they will be renamed. The *Ocean Princess* is to move to the UK in the fourth quarter of 2002 where she will be renamed *Oceana* to give the UK operation four very modern and large ships (*Aurora, Oriana, Arcadia,* and *Oceana*). The UK government has introduced a new. tonnage tax regime and companies are able to register in the UK and gain a financial benefit. For a traditional UK company, flying the red ensign of the UK mercantile fleet is of considerable bonus as it is a flag that carries more respect from customers than flags of convenience.

» *Improve cost efficiency.* As the business expands, the company intends to reduce unit costs through the integration of various functions and the realization of synergies and economies of scale within the global operations. There are many such economies of scale that can be realized – using the same port and terminal facilities for the different brands within the group, movement of staff across the group, group purchasing arrangements etc.

» *Consistency.* All P&O operations are carried out under the same logo, a flag bearing the royal colors of Spain and Portugal, the Iberian Peninsular countries. Even though P&O Princess Cruises has been a completely separate company since the demerger, quality standards under the same logo need to be consistent, even though the products are very different. P&O Scottish Ferries have operated a series of three-day mini-cruises on the scheduled services from Aberdeen to the Island groups of Orkney and Shetland in Scotland.

While these are small ships carrying both business, domestic and vacation traffic, the service standard on board is just as high as that on the *Aurora* or any other of the large cruise ships. Such consistency across a global operation is vital for success.

P&O made the transition from a traditional UK based company to a huge global operation at a time when the shipping industry appeared to be in decline. By merging local requirements with a corporate change from the liner to the cruise sector and by embracing containerization and ferry operations the company has built up a strong position and become an earner of vital foreign currency for the UK economy.

Fig. 7.2 shows a time line for P&O.

P&O – KEY INSIGHTS
» Ability and willingness to change to meet market demands
» Prepared to tailor products to meet local market requirements
» Consistency of standards across the global operation
» Use of both overt and covert expansion
» Keeping of well-known brand names
» Build up reputation over time.

SONY

Although he came from a family in the sake brewing business, Akio Morita had studied applied physics at university and then been a teacher until, late in World War II, he was commissioned as an officer in the Imperial Japanese Navy. His naval career did not last long as the two atomic bombs dropped by the Allies brought about the Japanese surrender in 1945.

Morita was not one to dwell on defeat and formed the Tokyo Telecommunications Engineering Company dealing in electrical components. He soon saw that a new piece of technology, the wire (later) tape recorder, would soon be an important feature of modern offices. By 1950 the company had produced its first machine and then found

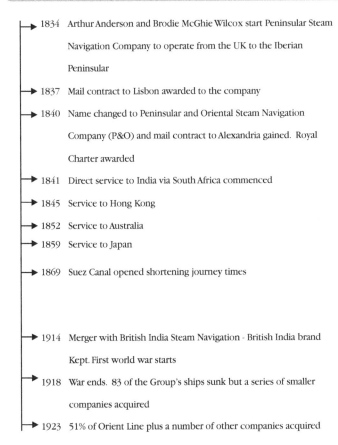

1834   Arthur Anderson and Brodie McGhie Wilcox start Peninsular Steam Navigation Company to operate from the UK to the Iberian Peninsular

1837   Mail contract to Lisbon awarded to the company

1840   Name changed to Peninsular and Oriental Steam Navigation Company (P&O) and mail contract to Alexandria gained. Royal Charter awarded

1841   Direct service to India via South Africa commenced

1845   Service to Hong Kong

1852   Service to Australia

1859   Service to Japan

1869   Suez Canal opened shortening journey times

1914   Merger with British India Steam Navigation - British India brand Kept. First world war starts

1918   War ends. 83 of the Group's ships sunk but a series of smaller companies acquired

1923   51% of Orient Line plus a number of other companies acquired

Fig. 7.2   Time line for P&O (for simplication this time line relates to the liner and cruise components of the company).

that very few Japanese knew what a tape recorder was and that thus there appeared to be no market. Morita set out to create a market by showing stenographers how useful this technology could be. He also showed how his machine could produce a Japanese soundtrack for English language instructional films both quickly and inexpensively.

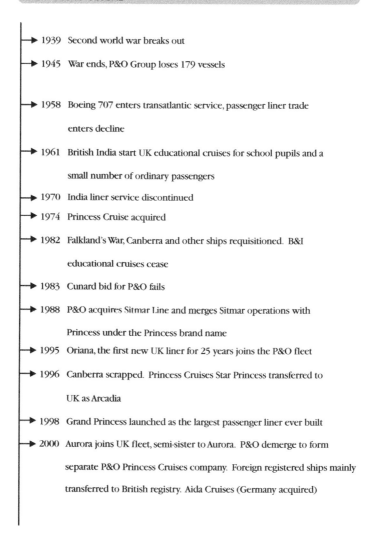

1939   Second world war breaks out

1945   War ends, P&O Group loses 179 vessels

1958   Boeing 707 enters transatlantic service, passenger liner trade

          enters decline

1961   British India start UK educational cruises for school pupils and a

          small number of ordinary passengers

1970   India liner service discontinued

1974   Princess Cruise acquired

1982   Falkland's War, Canberra and other ships requisitioned. B&I

          educational cruises cease

1983   Cunard bid for P&O fails

1988   P&O acquires Sitmar Line and merges Sitmar operations with

          Princess under the Princess brand name

1995   Oriana, the first new UK liner for 25 years joins the P&O fleet

1996   Canberra scrapped. Princess Cruises Star Princess transferred to

          UK as Arcadia

1998   Grand Princess launched as the largest passenger liner ever built

2000   Aurora joins UK fleet, semi-sister to Aurora. P&O demerge to form

          separate P&O Princess Cruises company. Foreign registered ships mainly

          transferred to British registry. Aida Cruises (Germany acquired)

Fig. 7.2   (*Continued*).

By 1952 Bell Laboratories in the US had developed the transistor, thus allowing for a considerable reduction in the size of electronic products. Morita made his first foray into international business by approaching Western Electric (the holders of Bell's patent) and negotiating a licensing agreement – the first stage in the strategic alliance system covered in Chapter 6.

In 1955 it was decided that a new, catchier name was needed for the company. The Latin *sonus,* meaning sound, was the starting point. It was sufficiently Western to appeal both in the West and in Japan and its root complemented the nature of the current products as they were sound related. Eventually Sony was decided upon. Short, easy to remember, and easy to pronounce.

By 1957 Sony were not only making tape recorders but had expanded into transistor radios. Their aim, not completely achieved, was to produce a radio small enough to fit in a pocket.

The company's first big international order was for 100,000 of these from the Bulova concern in New York, items that would be generic, i.e. made by Sony but with the Bulova brand attached. Morita did not want to be an OEM (original equipment manufacturer) and to everybody's surprise turned the order down. He intended that Sony would be a success based on its own brand name and not somebody else's. He was right, and soon Sony transistor radios were on sale in the US.

The product that launched the company onto the global stage was a derivative of the pocket radio concept – a tape recorder that only played back but was small enough for the owner to take their music around with them and not disturb anybody else. It is an anecdote common in marketing that culturally the Japanese used the "walkman" so as not to disturb anybody else while those in the west used it to listen to music in a manner that prevented the outside world disturbing them. True or not, there is no doubt that Sony created a market for the "walkman" as the product was branded. Many industry insiders believed that the product would flop if it had no recording system – who had heard of a tape recorder that would not record? Morita, however, refused to be deflected and was proved correct; as he stated, automobile stereo systems do not record and millions have been sold.

Morita also spent a great deal of time in the US, absorbing the culture and studying the market. The US, as the major world economy, is where products would be likely to take off first and so it has proved. Many countries resisted the influx of Japanese electronic products. For many years France only allowed imports through Poitiers (well inland) in an attempt to provide some protection to local manufacturers. However, the Japanese manufacturers, and Sony in particular, were offering inexpensive products designed and manufactured to a high standard.

The way around such restrictions was to set up Sony (France), Sony (Denmark) etc. In fact Sony has constantly sought alliances with indigenous companies as part of its expansion. In 1971 Sony commenced manufacturing in the US, in 1974 in the UK (where the company gained a Queen's Award for Industry on four occasions) and France in 1981–Sony were thus a local and a global company in an increasing number of areas. From their two UK factories (both in South Wales, a traditional mining area that has suffered high unemployment) Sony produce over one million TV sets for the UK and global markets.

When Sony acquired Columbia Pictures in 1989 they bought into another global industry, and the introduction of the popular Playstation® in 1994 gave the company an entry into the global advanced toy market.

In 2000 as the German government was preparing to move back to Berlin (the original German capital) from Bonn, Sony opened their new European headquarters in the Potsdamer Platz – a site considered by many to be the very center of Europe.

Today Sony makes many types of electrical products and has a worldwide reputation backed by local dealers and local servicing. Like the other successful global operations covered in this material, customers know that Sony is Japanese and yet that does not seem to matter. Sony's products are in fact global. They are items that people use all over the world and can thus be serviced all over the world.

The rebirth of the Japanese economy since 1945 has been miraculous but it owes that rebirth to people like Morita who were not isolationist and were prepared to find out what other markets required and then to find a way to satisfy those requirements. Morita died in 1999 aged 78 but has left a global legacy in that the name of the company he founded out of the ashes of the war is now part of the global language of both business and pleasure.

Fig. 7.3 shows a time line for Sony.

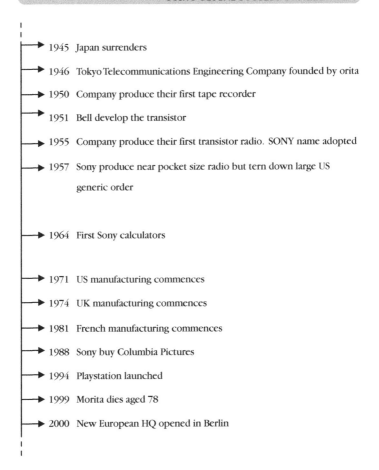

1945	Japan surrenders	
1946	Tokyo Telecommunications Engineering Company founded by orita	
1950	Company produce their first tape recorder	
1951	Bell develop the transistor	
1955	Company produce their first transistor radio. SONY name adopted	
1957	Sony produce near pocket size radio but tern down large US generic order	
1964	First Sony calculators	
1971	US manufacturing commences	
1974	UK manufacturing commences	
1981	French manufacturing commences	
1988	Sony buy Columbia Pictures	
1994	Playstation launched	
1999	Morita dies aged 78	
2000	New European HQ opened in Berlin	

Fig. 7.3 Time line for Sony.

SONY – KEY INSIGHTS

» Morita was able to create a market where one did not exist
» Licensing and joint agreements with foreign firms
» A careful study of the culture and market in areas where expansion was considered
» Products that met the needs of the market
» A commitment to quality
» A brand name that is easily remembered and neutral i.e. not especially Japanese.

Key Concepts and Thinkers

A glossary of the key terms and concepts of the global marketplace and globalization plus details of the key thinkers in the field:

- » Giddens
- » Harris, Philip and Moran
- » Hertz
- » Klein
- » Korten
- » Lewis
- » Porter
- » Trompenaars
- » Yip.

A GLOSSARY FOR GOING GLOBAL

CATIA (computer graphics-aided three-dimensional interactive application) – A computer design system used by Boeing for the design work on the Boeing 777. The system involved linking computers at Boeing with sub-contractors so that all staff had access to design changes etc.

Critical mass – The minimum size of an organization that enables it to operate successfully.

Culture – The values, attitudes, and beliefs ascribed to and accepted by a group, nation or organization. In effect, "the way we do things around here."

Design build teams (DBTs) – A Boeing term for the teams drawn from Boeing, their subcontractors and even customers responsible for the design etc. of a specific component on a product. DBTs were introduced for the design and building of the Boeing 777.

EPIC (electronic preassembly in the CATIA) – An extension to CATIA (see above) that allowed Boeing staff to study the interferences etc. in any designs, in effect building a virtual airplane.

Ethical investments – Investments made only in companies. Products, and countries that are approved on a value, and not an economic, basis by the investor.

European Union (EU) – The economic and, increasingly, political union between a number of European countries, formerly known as the European Economic Community (EEC).

Eurozone – Those EU countries that adopted a common currency, the Euro, on January 1, 2001. The UK has not yet joined the Eurozone and the subject is a matter of considerable political debate in the UK.

Export processing zones (EPZs) – Areas set up by governments (often in the developing world) where raw materials are imported and finished products manufactured and exported free of any customs duties.

Foreign Direct Investment (FDI) – The process whereby foreign companies either set up operations abroad or buy local companies and integrate them into their operations.

General Agreement on Tariffs and Trade (GATT) – Negotiations between countries to set the level of tariffs and encourage free trade. Superseded by the World Trade Organization (WTO) in 1994.

Globalization – The integration of the global economy by the dismantling of trade and political barriers and the increasing political and economic power of multinational corporations.

Global operation – Refers to an organization that operates on a worldwide basis and yet is integrated into the local community and economy.

Human resource management (HRM) – Often referred to as staffing or personnel management.

International Monetary Fund (IMF) – An international organization paid for by the nations of the world that acts as a lender of last resort to governments usually attaching strict public spending conditions on its loans.

International operation – Refers to organizations that operate worldwide but are clearly centered in their home country.

Local operation – Usually small/medium sized companies operating in a relatively small, closely defined local area.

National operation – Refers to the operations of a company confined to one country save for obtaining supplies.

North American Free Trade Agreement (NAFTA) – A free trade agreement between the US, Canada and Mexico.

Pan-national operation – Refers to an organization whose operations are confined to just two or three countries or within an economic bloc such as the EU or NAFTA.

Strategic alliance – Cooperation between companies, often across national borders. Such alliances may take the form of joint ventures and projects but are not mergers as each partner retains its independent identity.

World Trade Organization (WTO) – The organization that determines trading rules throughout the world and settles trading disputes between nations. Formed out of GATT in 1994.

KEY THINKERS

All of the books referred to in this section are listed fully in Chapter 9

Giddens, A.

Anthony Giddens is the Director of the London School of Economics and the pioneer of the ''Third Way'' concept between left and right wing that has been adopted by the UK Prime Minister, Tony Blair. In 1999 he was asked to present the BBC Reith Lecture and did so on the implications of globalization and the world becoming more homogenous. Challenging in its views, the lecture has now been produced in book form and makes fascinating reading as Giddens looks not only at business but also at traditions and the family etc. He also provides a superb reading list. Frequently consulted by heads of state, Giddens has written a large number of books on political and social themes that are outside the scope of this material.

Books:

» *Runaway World* (1999).

Harris, Philip and Moran, R.

US writers who have looked at how to manage across cultural differences within work and business. Theirs is well written work that takes a US perspective and provides examples of the differences between other cultures and that of the US. Their comments on the UK are particularly interesting and highlight some of the more subtle differences between two apparently closely related cultures. They have also stressed the importance of business leaders developing a global approach to modern business leadership.

Books:

» *Developing the Global Organization* (with W.G. Stripp) (1993)
» *Managing Cultural Differences*, 5th edition (2000)

Hertz, Noreena

Associate Director of the Centre for International Management at the Judge Institute of the University of Cambridge in the UK, Hertz has recently (2001) written *The Silent Takeover* in which she argues that global capitalism could cause the death of the very democracy that has allowed it to flourish. While the title might appear as a contradiction, as there are few corporate takeovers and mergers that are not reported widely in the media, the takeover Hertz refers to is of an altogether different order, referring to the takeover of the planet itself rather than a business rival, and "silent" because few have realized that it may be happening. She points out that of the world's largest economies, 51 are now corporations and only 49 are nation-states. Hertz has produced a highly readable account of economic change over the past two decades, an account her style makes highly readable. Hertz's view of globalization is that not everyone benefits from the capitalist dream and that CEOs often have more power than elected leaders. Hertz sees a time in the not too distant future when it is consumers' wallets that will decide policy and not the ballot box.

Her first book, *Russian Business Relationships in the Wake of Reform* was based upon a series of case studies of Russian enterprises that were tracked during the 1990s. It provides insight into the initial conditions that have been established in Russia, and which determine the kind of market system that is now emerging. This work also has a more general relevance and informs the broader theoretical debate on institutional and societal change that concerns not only Russia but elsewhere.

Books:

» *Russian Business Relationships in the Wake of Reform* (1997)
» *The Silent Takeover* (2001)

Klein, Naomi

Naomi Klein is a Canadian journalist and commentator who has been especially concerned with the effects of branding and globalization on society. In her book, *No Logo* (shortlisted for the *Guardian* First Book Award in 2000) she explores the effects of EPZs (see above) on the economies of countries such as the Philippines and argues that there appears to be little benefit to workers in such areas. She also examines the power of the consumer to make large organizations accountable. While mainly considering US based multi-nations, she also examines the behavior of Shell and other European operations. *No Logo* contains a useful reading list for those interested in studying globalization.

Books:

» *No Logo* (2000)

Magazine and journals:

» weekly column in the *Globe & Mail* (Canada)

Korten, David C.

The author of the best-selling *When Corporations Rule the World*, Korten addresses the issue of modern corporate power, exposing the harmful effects globalization is having not only on economics, but also on politics, society and the environment. His work documents the devastating consequences as corporations recreate values and institutions to serve their own and their stockholders' narrow financial interests. Korten outlines a strategy for creating localized economies that empower people and communities within a system of global cooperation. While his work is sometimes considered left-wing and controversial, Korten does attempt to put a model in place to remedy what he sees as the disastrous effects of globalization, and he has certainly enlivened and informed the debate by bringing it to a larger and more popular audience.

In *The Post Corporate World*, Korten examines the deep and growing gap between the promises of the new global capitalism and the reality of insecurity, inequality, social breakdown, spiritual emptiness, and environmental destruction which he believes that it leaves in its wake. The book looks at what went wrong and why, drawing on insights from the new biology and a growing human understanding of living systems to propose a solution – an economy that takes market principles seriously but also reflects the creativity and uniqueness of the individual. Korten also suggests specific actions to free the creative powers of individuals and societies through the realization of real democracy, the local rooting of capital through stakeholder ownership, and a restructuring of the rules of commerce to create market economies that combine market principles with a culture that nurtures social bonding and responsibility. This book is a useful complement to his earlier work – *Globalizing Civil Society*.

Books:

» *Getting to the 21st Century: Voluntary Action and the Global Agenda* (1990)

» *When Corporations Rule the World* (1995)
» *Globalizing Civil Society* (1997)
» *The Post Corporate World* (2000)

Lewis, Richard

Richard D. Lewis is an authority on the management of cultural difference. He is the founder of the magazine *Cross Culture* – of considerable interest to those involved in global expansion – can speak over 12 languages, and has worked with a large number of major multi-national organizations. Lewis makes the point that mutual understanding and sensitivity lie at the heart of managing across cultures. In both *When Cultures Collide* (2000), and *Cross-Cultural Communications: A Visual Approach* (1999), Lewis stresses the importance of ensuring that the communications process is as robust as possible. The same words and phrases can mean different things in different cultures and this is an important point to consider when the global organization is issuing policy documents etc.

Having developed a model for cultural analysis, Lewis has produced two PC-based packages, the first being "The Cross-Cultural Assessor" – a tool for cross-cultural analysis applicable to both individuals and across an organization – and the second, "Gulliver," which provides both cross-cultural training and a database to set up "what if scenarios." Details of Lewis's books and these products are given below and in Chapter 9.

Richard D. Lewis Communications and the associated Institute of Cross Cultural Communication (both based in the UK but operating globally) also produce a *Cross Cultural Letter to International Managers* ten times per year and available on subscription.

Books:

» *Cross-Cultural Communications: A Visual Approach* (1999)
» *When Cultures Collide* (2000)

Computer programs:

» "The Cross-Cultural Assessor" – this is a multimedia product designed to assist individuals and organizations in measuring, building and managing cross-cultural skills and characteristics.

» "Gulliver" – this is a computer-based training product – delivered either online or via CD-ROM and is a joint venture between Richard Lewis and PriceWaterhouseCoopers. The purpose of Gulliver is to help people involved in international business to perform successfully across cultures.

Porter, Michael

A renowned professor at Harvard Business School, Porter has been the world authority on competition and competitive strategies since the 1980s. His writing has informed both those in industry and academia on the nature of competition and the forces that drive the process. It was Porter who introduced the famous "Five Forces" model – the bargaining power of the supplier, the bargaining power of the customer, competition between existing players, the threat of new entrants and the treat of substitution – that has been used by many to explain how the competitive process has worked in particular industries. In the *Competitive Advantage of Nations* he turned his ideas and his attention to the global stage.

In this text he identified the fundamental determinants of national competitive advantage in an industry and how they work together to give international advantage. The findings had implications for firms and governments and set the agenda for discussions of global competition. The most relevant of his books for this material are listed below:

Books:

» *Competitive Advantage* (1980)
» *Cases in Competitive Strategy* (1982)
» *Competitive Strategy* (1985)
» *On Competition* (1998)
» *The Competitive Advantage of Nations* (1998) (new revised edition)

Trompenaars, Fons

Working originally in the Netherlands for Royal Dutch Shell, Fons Trompenaars has been one of the most influential writers on the management of cultural differences for global organizations. Shell as a global organization has considerable experience in managing different cultural groups and Trompenaars set out to put these experiences into a conceptual framework that could be transferred to other organizations. It is hard to find work on cultural diversity within the work situation and global operations that does not cite Trompenaars.

His initial work – *Riding the Waves of Culture: Understanding Cultural Diversity in Business*, published in 1993 was bought in large quantities by organizations operating on a global basis. The book not only provided a contextual framework but also provided concrete examples of the differing cultural norms that managers were likely to encounter and strategies for dealing with them in a sensitive and effective manner.

In association with Charles Hampden-Turner, Trompenaars looked in more detail at the competencies required for cross-cultural management (*Building Cross-cultural Competence*, 2000) and the requirements for twenty-first century business leaders in a more globalized environment (*21 Leaders for the 21st Century*, 2001) as well as a detailed examination of social, cultural and economic differences between Asia and the west in *Mastering the Infinite Game* (1997).

The cultural attributes considered by Trompenaars are:

» Attitude to time
» Universal vs. particular
» Individualism vs. collectivism
» Emotional vs. neutral
» Specific vs. diffuse
» Achievement vs. ascription
» Attitudes to the environment.

and were first described by Trompenaars with specific examples of each related to a series of different cultures to show how a similar scenario may well be dealt with in very varying ways.

Fons Trompenaars is recommended reading for all those dealing with global expansion, blending as he does practical advice within a useful conceptual framework.

Books:

» *Riding the Waves of Culture* (1997)
» *Mastering the Infinite Game* (with C. Hampden-Turner) (1997)

» *Building Cross Cultural Competence* (with C. Hampden-Turner) (2000)
» *21 Leaders for the 21st Century* (with C. Hampden-Turner) (2001)

Yip, George S.

A teacher of business strategy and international marketing at UCLA and a former faculty member at Harvard Business School, Yip has written a useful guide on the processes involved in going global in *Total Global Strategy*. Very much concerned with the gaining of competitive advantage, Yip provides clear practical advice on global marketing, product design, competition and the structure of a global organization.

Well qualified to comment on global organizations as he is Asian by birth, lives in the US, and has EU citizenship, Yip has also written on developing strategies for Central and Eastern European expansion and on expanding into Asian markets.

Books:

» *Total Global Strategy* (1992)
» *Strategies for Central and Eastern Europe* (with A. Kozminski – editor) (2000)
» *Asian Advantage* (2000)

Resources for Going Global

Where to find resources for the study of the global market and globalization:

» Books
» Journals and magazines
» Websites.

BOOKS

Note: Dates of books in this chapter may differ from those shown in previous chapters. The dates here are of editions that have been revised from the date of first publication as shown in the chapter material.

Bower, T. (2000), *Branson*, London, 4th Estate.

Cartwright, R. (2001), *Mastering the Business Environment*, Palgrave, Basingstoke.

Cartwright, R. (2001), *Managing Diversity*, Capstone, Oxford.

Collier, P. and Horowitz, D. (1976), *The Rockefellers: An American Dynasty*, Simon & Schuster, New York.

Davies, C. (1997), *Divided by a Common Language*, Mayflower Press, Sarasota, FL.

Eddy, P., Potter, E. and Page, B. (1976), *Destination Disaster*, Hart–Davis, London.

Ellwood, W. (2001), *The No-nonsense Guide to Globalization*, New Internationalist, Oxford.

Foot, D.K. and Stoffman, D. (1996), *Boom, Bust and Echo*, Macfarlane, Walter & Ross, Toronto.

Giddens, A. (1999), *Runaway World*, Profile Books, London.

Harris, P.R. and Moran, R.T. (2000), *Managing Cultural Differences*, Gulf Publishing Co., Houston.

Heinecke, W.E. and Marsh, J. (2000), *The Entrepreneur-21 Golden Rules for the Global Business Manager*, John Wiley & Sons (Asia), Singapore.

Hertz, N. (1997), *Russian Business Relationships in the Wake of Reform*, Palgrave, Basingstoke.

Hertz, N. (2001), *The Silent Takeover*, Heinemann, London.

Jones, J.W. (1999), *Virtual Entrepreneurs: Electronic Commerce in the 21st Century*, BPRI, Rosemont.

Jones, T.O. and Strasser, W.E. Jr (1995), "Why Satisfied Customers Defect," *Harvard Business Review*, Nov.-Dec., pp. 88–99.

Joynt, P. and Morton, R. (eds) (1999), *The Global HR Manager*, Chartered Institute of Personnel and Development, London.

Klein, N. (2000), *No Logo*, Flamingo, London.

Korten, D.C. (1990), *Getting to the 21st Century: Voluntary Action and the Global Agenda*, Kumarian Press, New York.

Korten, D.C. (1996), *When Corporations Rule the World*, Berrett-Koehler, San Francisco.

Korten, D.C. (1997), *Globalizing Civil Society*, Seven Stories Press, New York.

Korten, D.C. (1999), *The Post Corporate World*, Berrett-Koehler, San Francisco.

Lewis, R.D. (1999), *Cross Cultural Communications: A Visual Approach*, Transcreen, London.

Lewis, R.D. (2000), *When Cultures Collide*, Nicholas Brealey, London.

Lorange, P. and Roos, J. (1992), *Strategic Alliances*, Blackwell USA, Cambridge, MA.

Lynn, M. (1995), *Birds of Prey – Boeing v Airbus*, Heinemann, London.

Marquardt, M.J. and Berger, N.O. (2000), *Global Leaders for the 21st Century*, State University of New York Press, Albany.

Moran, R.T., Harris, P.R. and Stripp, W.G. (1998), *Developing the Global Organization: Strategies for Human Resource Professionals*, Gulf Publishing Co., Houston.

Morita, A. (1986), *Made in Japan*, HarperCollins, New York.

Nicholson, M. (2000), *Managing the Human Animal*, Crown, New York.

Pascale, R. and Athos, A. (1981), *The Art of Japanese Management*, Simon & Schuster, New York.

Pendergrast, M. (2000), *For God, Country, and Coca-Cola*, Orion, London.

Peters, T. and Waterman, R. (1982), *In Search of Excellence*, Harper & Row, New York.

Porter, M. (1980), *Competitive Advantage*, Free Press, New York.

Porter, M. (1992), *Cases in Competitive Strategy*, Free Press, New York.

Porter, M. (1985), *Competitive Strategy*, Free Press, New York.

Porter, M. (1996), *On Competition*, Harvard Business School Press, Cambridge, MA.

Porter, M. (1998), *The Competitive Advantage of Nations*, Macmillan, Basingstoke.

Price, C. (2000), *The Internet Entrepreneurs*, Pearson, Harlow.

Ransom, D. (2001), *The No-nonsense Guide to Fair Trade*, New Internationalist, Oxford.

Trompenaars, F. (1993), *Riding the Waves of Culture: Understanding Cultural Diversity in Business*, Economist Books, London.

Trompenaars, F. and Hampden-Turner, C. (1997), *Mastering the Infinite Game*, Capstone, Oxford.

Trompenaars, F. and Hampden-Turner, C. (2000), *Building Cross Cultural Competence*, Wiley, Chichester.

Trompenaars, F. and Hampden-Turner, C. (2001), *21 Leaders for the 21st Century*, Capstone, Oxford.

United Nations (1999), *Human Development Report*, UN Development Program/Oxford University Press, Oxford.

Yip, G.S. (1992), *Total Global Strategy*, Prentice Hall, Englewood Cliffs, NJ.

Yip, G.S. (2000) *The Asian Advantage: Key Strategies for Winning in the Asia-Pacific Region Updated Edition – After the Crisis*, Perseus Books.

Yip, G.S. and Kozminski, A.K. (eds) (2000), *Strategies for Central and Eastern Europe*, Palgrave, Basingstoke.

For information about Amazon.com

Saunders, R. (2000), *Amazon.com*, Capstone, Oxford.

Spector, R. (2000), *Amazon.com: Get Big Fast*, Random House, London.

For information about Body Shop

Roddick, A. (2000), *Business as Usual*, HarperCollins, London.

For information about Boeing and the 777

Sabbach, K. (1995), *21st Century Jet: The Making of the Boeing 777*, Macmillan, Basingstoke.

For Information about the British East India Company

Wild, A. (2000), *The East India Company*, Collins, London.

For information about the EU and the Social Charter

Pettinger, R. (1998), *The European Social Charter: A Manager's Guide*, Kogan Page, London.

For information on the Internet

Aldrich, D.F. (1999), *Mastering the Digital Marketplace*, New York, John Wiley.

For information about Microsoft and Bill Gates

Manes, S. and Andrews, P. (1994), *Gates*, Simon & Schuster, New York.

Dearlove, D. (2001), *Doing Business the Bill Gates Way*, Capstone, Oxford.

For information on J P Morgan

Davie, M. (1986), *Titanic: The Full Story of a Tragedy*, Bodley Head, London.

Gardiner, R. and Van der Vat, D. (1995), *The Riddle of the Titanic*, Weidenfeld & Nicolson, London.

Strouse, J. (2000), *Morgan: An American Financier*, Harper Perennial, New York.

For information about cruising and P&O

Cartwright, R. and Baird, C. (1999), *The Development and Growth of the Cruise Industry*, Butterworth Heinemann, Oxford.

Dickinson, R. and Vladimir, A. (1997), *Selling the Sea*, Wiley, New York.

P&O (1995), *Oriana: From Dream to Reality*, P&O, London.

P&O (2000), *Aurora: Dawn of a New Era*, P&O, London.

Ward, D. (2000), *The Berlitz Guide to Cruising and Cruise Ships 2001*, Berlitz, Princeton, NJ.

Williams, D.L. (1998), *P&O*, Ian Allan, Shepperton.

For information about Sony and Akio Morita

Morita, A. (1994), *Made in Japan*, HarperCollins, London.

For information about the Suez and Panama Canals

McCullough, D. (1977), *The Path Between the Seas*, Simon & Schuster, New York.

MAGAZINES AND JOURNALS

Those interested in global expansion etc. should consult the quality newspapers of the areas/countries in which they are interested. Major western broadsheet type newspapers, e.g. *The Washington Post, New York Times, Herald Tribune, London Times, Daily Telegraph, Observer, Le Monde* etc., provide useful analysis of news and financial/business matters and cover international, in addition to national, news. Current affairs and other relevant programs on the radio or television are useful, but as with newspapers a translator may be required. Most major newspapers now have an online edition.

The following, most of which are published online as well as in hard copy (see web sites at the end of this chapter), are useful sources of information about markets, competitors, and developments. The web sites should be accessed for subscription rates, samples, and special subscription offers.

Business 2.0

Business and financial daily newspaper carrying articles etc. of an international nature. The importance of scanning such material for items of possible interest cannot be overstated.

Economist

Weekly current affairs magazine with a global approach and thus very useful. *The Economist* carries general current affairs news in addition to analysis and market news on a global basis. Issued both as a print version and online. Available by subscription or from news stands.

Forbes

Forbes is a leading company providing resources for the world's business and investment leaders, providing them with commentary, analysis, relevant tools and real-time reporting; includes real-time original reporting on business, technology, investing and lifestyle. Forbes is extremely useful reading for all those involved with global business.

The weekly *Forbes* magazine is also available online and while mainly designed for a US audience is read on a global basis. *Forbes* often carries articles and commentaries on entrepreneurs and entrepreneurial activities. Other linked products from Forbes include:

» *Forbes Global*: covering the rise of capitalism around the world for international business leaders. Contains sections on companies and industry, capital markets and investing, entrepreneurs, technology and *Forbes Global Life*.

» Forbes Newsletters including:

Forbes Aggressive Growth Investor, a monthly newsletter recommending the 50 best growth and momentum stocks to own now as determined by a proprietary multi-dimensional computer analysis of over 3000 stocks.

Gilder Technology Report covering the smartest, most profitable way to invest in technology.

Special Situation Survey with monthly stock recommendations, hold or sell advice on each recommendation and special investment reports – tends to be of interest mainly to investors in the US, of which there are many in Europe and Asia.

New Economy Watch: a newsletter that looks at Internet-based companies.

Time

Time Magazine, while originally a US product, has a global readership and is one of the most important current affairs and commentary magazines in existence. To appear on the cover of *Time* is to have made it; to be the *Time* man/woman of the year is a considerable honor indeed.

Time covers a huge range of issues and is thus a useful tool for those involved in global expansion. The print version is available either on subscription or from news stands.

Time was the first news magazine to publish online, beginning in 1993 and launched TIME.com in 1994. According to Nielsen NetRatings, TIME.com is the most trafficked news magazine site online. TIME.com draws over 5 million visits per month and receives over 32 million monthly page views. The site covers the events impacting the world each day and offers its own perspective on the latest news. There are also sections entitled: Nation, Education, World, and Health.

LIFEmag.com looks at the defining moments and great events of our lives through photography. The site features a Picture of the Day, This Day in LIFE and a searchable magazine and cover collection dating back to 1936. ONmagazine.com is the online complement to ON, the million-plus monthly personal-tech magazine from the editors of *Time*. The site is a before-you-buy authority on new gadgets and web services. ONmagazine.com features a new hands-on review every weekday, along with jargon-free how-to-buy guides for popular product categories.

TRADE AND PROFESSIONAL JOURNALS

Each company operates in its own sectors and particular marketplace with a set of product, services or ideas unique to the sector to at least some extent. In addition to understanding the general world of business and commerce there will be specific sectoral requirements and knowledge that the company needs to consider.

Nearly every occupation, profession and business sector has journals and magazines dedicated to it and often related to the concerns of a specific country. These can normally be acquired by interested parties and provide an insight into the particular professional trade issues in that area.

In addition to the written word there are trade and professional associations across the globe dealing with nearly every type of business activity. Membership may well be worth while but it is worth remembering that such organizations exist to exchange information – there will be a requirement to give as well as to take. If a company is planning a covert move, it may well not be wise to join such an association before all the deals are done.

GOVERNMENT PUBLICATIONS

Governments across the globe produce a wealth of statistics and other useful information that can usually be acquired via their network of embassies and consulates, all of which will be listed in local telephone directories. In addition, virtually every government in the world has an official web site that can be found using a normal search engine.

WEBSITES

- » www.amazon.com – Amazon.com main Website
- » www.amazon.co.uk – Amazon UK Website
- » www.business2.com – Business 2 Website

» www.corpwatch.org – Globalization ''watchdog'' network
» www.economist.com – Economist Website
» www.europa.eu.int – European Union Website
» www.forbes.com – Forbes Website
» www.nafta.customs.org – NAFTA Website
» www.odci.gov/cia/publications/factbook/index.html
»   – (World Fact Book – CIA/USA)
» www.open.gov.uk – (UK public sector information)
» www.poprincesscruises.com – P&O Princess Cruises Website
» www.sony.com – Sony Website
» www.statistics.gov.uk – (UK Government Office of National Statistics)
» www.time.com – Time Magazine Website

Sample Websites for Mexico (see Chapter 5)

» www.mib.org.mx – Mexican Investment Board Website
» www.latinvestor.com/country/mexico.htm – Latin America investment site
» www.mexconnect.com/mex – Mexico Connect – assisting companies to develop commercial links with Mexico

Ten Steps to Assist Going Global

The ten key steps that a company/organization going global needs to consider are:

1 Analyze the market and the environment for opportunities
2 Decide whether expansion is to be overt or covert
3 Consider who the customers will be
4 Consider what the competition will be
5 Find out what assistance is available
6 Become knowledgeable about the culture
7 Decide on a marketing strategy
8 Train the staff, both new and existing
9 Tie the operation into other company activities
10 Make the operation seem indigenous.

As has been mentioned in this material, modern Internet technology can allow even the smallest business to cater for a global customer base or to resource supplies etc. from a wide geographic area. Thus the steps below can be applied across the whole range of companies from the smallest to the largest and are independent of the business sector. The first step should be noted carefully because precisely how the organization goes global will be contingent upon the results of the analysis of the external environment that it carries out.

1. ANALYZE THE MARKET AND THE ENVIRONMENT FOR OPPORTUNITIES

No company should consider any form of expansion without firstly analyzing the market for opportunities. A complete analysis should include a consideration of the SPECTACLES factors (Cartwright, 2001 – *Mastering the Business Environment*) consisting of Social, Political, Economic, Cultural, Technological, Aesthetic, Customers, Legal, Environmental and Sectoral factors. Sectoral analysis also includes an analysis of the commercial competition likely to be encountered.

It is only after analysis that the likelihood of a successful expansion can be assessed. Company executives should never be afraid to say "no" to an expansion if analysis shows that there might be problems. On the other hand the company that takes no risks is likely to make no major commercial progress. It is all a question of balancing the threats and opportunities. If the latter outweigh the former, then the expansion may well be in the company's interests.

2. OVERT OR COVERT?

Decide whether the expansion should be overt or covert. Are the company's brands and products well known enough to be recognized and be sought after or should a local company and its brands together with its customers be acquired?

3. WHO ARE THE CUSTOMERS?

Any company moving into a new area whether nationally or globally should carry out market research to find out precisely what are the potential customer's needs and wants. It may be that these differ from area to area. Such market research may be costly but the costs of not carrying it out are nearly always greater. Chapter 6 and the P&O case study in Chapter 7 should be consulted on this point. It is such research that will show whether cosmetic differences will be acceptable to existing products or whether major design changes are necessary.

4. WHO ARE THE COMPETITION?

According to Michael Porter, "the guru of competitiveness" (see Chapter 8), there are three main types of competition operating in a market: competition from existing players, competition from new entrants and competition from substitutes. The latter are products and services that can act as substitutes for the traditional method of satisfying customer needs and wants. For example, up to the opening of the Channel Tunnel between the UK and France in the 1990s, the competition from passengers and freight was between the ferry operators and the airlines as flying or a sea journey were the only methods of making the journey. Once the Channel Tunnel was opened, rail travel was able to act as a substitute for the traditional means. While the journey was longer than from airport to airport it was actually quicker when measured from city center to city center and Eurostar, as the service is known between London and Paris/Brussels, soon gained a respectable market share.

Where ever possible the company should sample its potential and actual competitors' products/services and compare them against its own for price, quality, ease of use, convenience of purchase etc.

5. WHAT ASSISTANCE IS AVAILABLE?

Many governments are only too happy to provide assistance to a company wishing to relocate onto their territory. Relocating companies, it is hoped, will provide employment and allow for technology to be transferred. The more people are earning, the more taxes they pay and thus any organization offering employment is usually welcomed. The setting up of EPZs (see Chapters 5 and 8) have been a characteristic of many developing countries. Even national and local government in developed countries may offer infrastructure and training grants plus relief from corporate or property taxes in order to entice jobs to an area. As with all supply and demand, the greatest assistance is usually available in those areas where unemployment is high. An example of useful websites in respect of Mexico is provided in Chapter 9.

6. BECOME KNOWLEDGEABLE ABOUT THE CULTURE

Once a decision to expand into an area has been decided, all those involved must ensure that they understand the culture they will be entering into. It is that culture that will dictate employee and customer behavior. Without taking cultural factors into account the whole enterprise is starting off without the prime requirement for success – understanding the people who will make it a success.

7. DECIDE ON A MARKETING STRATEGY

Different cultures and areas require different means of putting the message across to the potential customer base. Taking promotional, advertising and marketing concepts from one culture and using them in another may not work. Humor, often used as a marketing tool can travel very badly.

Useful tools to put across a company and its brands are competitions and sponsorship. Commercial organizations often sponsor national competitions, often involving children and sporting/cultural events. Using these mediums can put the name of the company/brands in front of a large audience in a ''non-selling'' and therefore less pushy way.

8. TRAINING

Moving into a new area will require the employment of local staff. These staff need to be trained before operations commence and products/services are released to the customers. Training should never be treated as an expense – it is an investment. A well-trained staff repays the investment many fold. An untrained staff lose the company customers – customers who may well go to a competitor. It is also a good early opportunity to introduce newly appointed local staff to the company and its corporate culture and to start relationships with local educational establishments. It may also be necessary to train existing staff elsewhere about the culture in the area of the new operation.

9. TIE THE OPERATION INTO OTHER COMPANY ACTIVITIES

Consistency of product and delivery is important for global organizations. There should never be a difference in quality between products from one area and another. Neither should service standards differ.

Global companies are successful because of the seamless web of operations that they present. As will be considered in the next step, this seamless web means that they belong to the local area but also to the whole world.

It is also important to set prices at such a level as to maximize local sales but not make customers elsewhere dissatisfied. This can cause the problem of parallel importing covered in Chapter 6.

10. MAKE THE OPERATION SEEM INDIGENOUS

The world knows that Coca-Cola, Ford and Kellogg are US companies and yet in the areas where they operate and manufacture they are also considered to be local/national organizations. Customers are more likely to patronize a local supplier than a foreign one. By becoming an integral part of the community and showing that they actually care about the local environment and its people, the successful global company can at the same time span the world and yet be considered local. This will not occur overnight as a company needs to be in an area for some time before it is considered as an integral part of the landscape and yet it is well worth the effort as this aids motivation and customer loyalty.

KEY LEARNING POINTS

Organizations cannot move into a new area without:

» Analyzing the environment
» Analyzing the culture

» Considering the customer base
» Considering existing competition
» Finding out who can assist
» Maintaining consistency.

Frequently Asked Questions (FAQs)

Q1: How important is it to conduct an analysis of the market?

A: It is of vital importance. Without a clear knowledge of all the factors that influence the way a particular market operates and its relationship with its external environment it is very difficult to plan an effective entry strategy. There is more about this aspect of going global in Chapter 6.

Q2: How important is it to understand the culture of the area into which the company wishes to expand?

A: Culture determines people's behavior. Customers, staff, suppliers, government officials will all behave according to their cultural norms. Advertising needs to be such as to respect the culture and not put across an offensive or misleading message. There are resources available, as covered in Chapter 9, to assist in ensuring that the company presents the right cultural message and image.

Q3: Are variations to standard products and services always necessary?

A: Sometimes a standard product requires very little change. Nike sneakers or Benneton products are cases in point; they appear to be globally accepted in a standard format. Software products such as Microsoft Windows® need to be adapted to local languages (most modern software products are so equipped as part of the package). Automobiles need to be either left or right-hand drive. North America and Europe have traditionally used different forms of television and videocassette systems although the latest generation of VCRs (video-cassette recorders) can recognize both. Electrical outlets in the US are 120 volts while in Europe they are 240 volts, meaning that transformers and adapters are required if a US market machine is used in Europe (most laptop computers come with the necessary adapters that can read both voltages as do electric razors). Even within Europe there are a number of national types of electrical plugs – for many years there have been discussions about standardization but as yet there has been little progress especially in persuading the UK to change from its system.

There may be national standards connected with quality and safety to be taken into consideration.

Many of the changes may be to the peripherals such as plugs etc., and modern production techniques are well equipped to deal with these.

Measurement systems and sizes may also differ requiring different labels to be added to the product. See Chapters 6 and 7 for further details on local variations.

Q4: Where does one find out about relocation assistance when planning to go global?

A: Most governments will have an agency, usually a branch of their trade and industry department (however it might be titled), that provides advice and assistance on relocation. As an example, Chapter 9 provides the web addresses of three sites that might be of interest to companies considering a move into Mexico. Useful information may also be available from organizations such as NAFTA and the EU (see Chapter 9). A consideration of EPZs etc. is provided in Chapter 5.

Q5: How should the company market itself and its brands when going global?

A: Marketing often has to be country or region specific in order to avoid language and cultural problems. Competitions and sponsorship can be useful tools for companies to put their name forward to a large audience and show that they are trying to put something into society as well as taking it out. One has only to see the success of Coca-Cola in assisting in the finances of the Tokyo Olympics and their subsequent growth in Japan to see how beneficial such activities can be. The beneficial aspects of globalization are covered in Chapter 5.

Q6: How can the Internet and modern technology assist companies and organizations that are going global?

A: The use of e-mail and videoconferencing can speed up the communications process and ensure that information is readily available to all parts of the operation. It can also aid networking by bringing people from across the company together without the need to travel.

The Internet can also allow even the smallest company to reach a global customer base. More details of the role of Internet in going global are given in Chapter 4.

Q7: Is globalization always considered in negative terms and as a threat to democracy?

A: There are those who believe that the democratic unaccountability of large multi-national organizations is dangerous to democracy. There is also a view that just moving from one low wage economy does nothing to help ordinary people in those areas. Companies are accountable to those who own them – normally the stock/shareholders and are in business to make money. Governments have a responsibility to ensure that their citizens are not exploited. Many governments provide large incentives to encourage relocation. The anti-globalization lobby's argument is that the large company with money can dictate to an impoverished government. Globalization is a growing trend, however, and if governments and companies work together it can act to strengthen democracy and raise standards of living. There is more detail on globalization in Chapter 5.

Q8: Does the growth of globalization mean that there is no place for local companies?

A: There will always be a place for local companies especially in the service sector. What those companies cannot rely on is a customer base that is a hostage to them. They will have to add their own unique selling points, examples being speed of delivery, local knowledge etc. in order to compete. There will also be niche markets that the global organizations will not be interested in. The process of going global is considered in Chapter 6 and the use of the Internet by smaller, local companies in Chapter 4.

Q9: Is it really possible to present a local and a global image at the same time?

A: It is doing this that has made companies such as Coca-Cola and Ford the success that they are. To many in the UK, Ford is a British automobile manufacture, the same is true of other areas where Ford has plants – the company is considered an integral part of the local/national economy. Yet Ford is a major US company and everybody knows that – the dichotomy is one that promotes success. Global companies need to appear local if they are to engender loyalty.

Q10: Where are resources available to assist in understanding the process of going global and globalization?

A: A list of books, journals and web addresses can be found in Chapter 9.

Index